HOMEGROWN

CULTIVATING *kids* IN THE FRUIT OF THE SPIRIT

DR. JOSH & CHRISTI STRAUB

LifeWay Press® Nashville, Tennessee

Published by LifeWay Press®
© 2019 Dr. Josh and Christi Straub

No part of this book may be reproduced or transmitted in any form
or by any means, electronic or mechanical, including photocopying
and recording, or by any information storage or retrieval system,
except as may be expressly permitted in writing by the publisher.
Requests for permission should be addressed in writing to LifeWay
Press®; One LifeWay Plaza; Nashville, TN 37234.

ISBN: 978-1-5359-5015-2
Item: 005813576
Dewey decimal classification: 248.84
Subject heading: HOLY SPIRIT / SPIRITUAL FORMATION /
                            SPIRITUAL LIFE

Unless otherwise noted, all Scripture quotations are taken from
the Christian Standard Bible®, Copyright © 2017 by Holman Bible
Publishers®. Used by permission. Christian Standard Bible® and
CSB® are federally registered trademarks of Holman Bible Publishers.
Scripture quotations from THE MESSAGE. Copyright © by Eugene
H. Peterson 1993, 1994, 1995, 1996, 2000, 2001, 2002. Used by
permission of NavPress. All rights reserved. Represented by Tyndale
House Publishers, Inc.

To order additional copies of this resource, write LifeWay Church
Resources Customer Service; One LifeWay Plaza; Nashville, TN
37234; Fax order to 615.251.5933; call toll-free 800.458.2772; email
orderentry@lifeway.com; order online at www.lifeway.com; or visit
the LifeWay Christian Store serving you.

Printed in Canada.

Adult Ministry Publishing, LifeWay Church Resources,
One LifeWay Plaza, Nashville, TN 37234

**EDITORIAL TEAM,
ADULT MINISTRY
PUBLISHING**

Michelle Hicks
Manager, Adult Ministry
Short Term Bible Studies

Elizabeth Hyndman
Content Editor

Lindsey Bush
Production Editor

Heather Wetherington
Art Director

Chelsea Waack
Graphic Designer

Alexis Ward
Cover Design

Contents

About the Authors

Josh Straub

Josh Straub, Ph.D., cherishes his role as husband and dad. A champion of human empathy, Josh leads Famous at Home, a company equipping leaders, organizations, military families, and churches in emotional intelligence and family wellness. Josh also is a Fellow of the Townsend Institute for Leadership and Counseling. As a marriage and family coach and consultant with The Straub Co., and professor of child psychology/crisis response, Josh coaches leaders to be famous at home so they can thrive on their stage. He also speaks regularly for Joint Special Operations Command and serves military families across the country.

Josh is author/coauthor of four books including *Safe House: How Emotional Safety Is the Key to Raising Kids Who Live, Love, and Lead Well* and coauthor, along with his wife Christi, of their first children's book called, *What Am I Feeling?* (B&H Kids, 2019). He and Christi also host the *In This Together* podcast, and in partnership with LifeWay Christian Resources, are the creators of *22:6 Parenting*, a community of parents growing together to encourage the spiritual growth of their kids.

Christi Straub

Christi Straub, M.A., M.B.A., is a native Canadian, wife to an American, and momma to two feisty kiddos. She is a marriage and family coach and leads The Straub Co., an organization where she and her husband, Josh, coach families to live, love, and lead well. Christi is a Fellow of the Townsend Institute for Leadership and Counseling. Her honesty, wittiness, and transparency are contagious. She is co-host of the *In This Together* podcast and is coauthor of the children's book, *What Am I Feeling?* (B&H Kids, 2019).

When she and Josh aren't working together, they spend time on the lake on their 1974 Crestliner, train their disobedient puppy, and watch their kids crush karaoke on a stage built in their dining room.

Introduction

We want to begin by stressing how incredibly grateful we are for parents who have a desire to cultivate the fruit of the Spirit in their kids. You've been given a unique privilege and responsibility to disciple them in the ways of the Lord.

But that's easier said than done. You don't have to be a parent for long to feel like, in some way, you're already messing up. That's why we want to begin by assuring you, if you feel inadequate, you're not alone. Many of us didn't grow up in homes with parents who discipled us, let alone taught us about the Holy Spirit. On the other hand, what an amazing encouragement it is to begin a legacy of modeling for your kids the love for the Scriptures and our great God. There's nothing more important. With that said, here are a few things to keep in mind as you cultivate the fruit of the Spirit in your children.

1. We were not meant to teach our children alone. Moses wrote in Deuteronomy 6 the best way to instill the love and commands of God onto the hearts of our kids. But he wasn't just speaking to parents. He was speaking to Israel as a whole. Today that would be like addressing the entire church. In other words, when you need help, or have a question, don't be afraid to ask. You can talk to your pastor, another close friend, or an older couple in your church you look up to. Whomever it is you admire, seek them out. We're in this together.

2. As you navigate your way through the study, keep in mind that not all children learn the same way. Developmentally, our kids are unlikely to be on the same emotional or spiritual level. Understanding each child individually helps us know how we can best disciple them. We want our kids to be interested in what they learn. Keep it fun!

3. Keep in mind that the goal of discipling our children is not just to help them learn the truths of the Bible but to also apply these truths in how they live their lives, especially with how they treat others. We believe wholeheartedly that spiritual maturity and emotional maturity go hand-in-hand.

4. Which leads us to our last point—one that cannot be understated. As parents, the best way to cultivate our kids in the fruit of the Spirit is to be growing in the fruit of the Spirit ourselves. Never be shy about sharing with your child what God is teaching you from His Word. We have to tell them—and more importantly—show them by our fruit.

Walking Alongside You!

Christi + Josh

How to Use This Study

This study may be a little different from other studies you've done because it's meant to be a study for your whole family. Each week, you'll find a group discussion guide, a parent study guide, applications, and family activities. While they are labeled as "Day 1," "Day 2," and so on, we do not want you to feel rushed or guilty if you are not able to do the study in that time frame. Have grace for yourself and your children as you grow together. This study is meant to cultivate the fruit of the Spirit in you as you, in turn, help cultivate those fruit in your children.

Group Discussion Guide

If you meet with a small group of other parents, use these questions to guide your discussion. We've placed them after the week of study so you can discuss what you learned throughout the week, what worked for your kids, and what didn't. These questions are optional—meant to be used as a guide instead of a to-do list. Allow discussion to vary as needed to encourage and challenge the parents involved.

If you would like to meet before beginning the study to introduce the topic and meet other parents, use the following as a guide for discussion:

Tell us about your family. What are your kids' names and ages?

Read Galatians 5:16-25 aloud.

What do you know about the fruit of the Spirit?

What do you hope to learn and gain from this study of the fruit of the Spirit?

What's your biggest challenge in teaching your kids to walk in the Holy Spirit?

What does it look like to keep in step with the Spirit personally? In your family?

Pray together as a group, that you all might be encouraged this week as you learn more about the fruit of the Spirit. Pray for your families, that they will be open to the time spent in God's Word.

Parent Study Guide

These pages are for you, as parents, to learn a little more about each fruit of the Spirit while reflecting on how this fruit shows up in your life and the lives of your children. We hope these questions, examples, and Scriptures will deepen your study of the Holy Spirit and the way of life for believers. You can complete these pages alone or with your spouse.

Application and Family Activities

We suggest you set up a weekly "Homegrown time" for the entire family—a time you plan to gather and discuss what you're learning and do the family activities suggested in this book. We also know that children are often on different spiritual, intellectual, and emotional levels within one home, so you may want to take advantage of one of four key times of the day (waking up, drive time, dinner time, and bedtime). We've made suggestions for how to discuss the fruit of the Spirit during those key times throughout this study. This can be a more one-on-one approach, which will provide your child the opportunity to ask questions or share thoughts and concerns they may not want their siblings to hear.

Understanding My Child

Each week, you'll find a page with some practical tips for teaching your child biblical truths and Bible skills. We hope these will be a helpful learning tool for all ages, with the parents learning right alongside their kids!

Optional Videos

Want more coaching, tips, and practical help from Dr. Josh + Christi? Watch the free coaching videos for each fruit of the Spirit at 226Parenting.com/HomegrownVideos.

THE FRUIT OF THE

Spirit

IS LOVE, JOY, PEACE,

patience,

KINDNESS, GOODNESS,

faithfulness,

GENTLENESS, AND

self-control.

GALATIANS 5:22-23

SESSION 1: THE FOUNDATION FOR FRUIT

As parents, the thought of cultivating our children in the fruit of the Spirit can feel like a pipe dream some days. Busyness creeps in. Tempers flare. Just getting our kids into bed sometimes feels like a massive parenting win.

And now I'm expected to get my son to be kind? And my daughter to have self-control? My children just watched me lose self-control and snap at my spouse.

We get it. That's our story too. We feel like we're starting from behind, like there's no way it could happen. Here's the good news: You're not alone. You have the Holy Spirit's help. In fact, none of us can grow these supernatural qualities on our own willpower.

And guess what? You *will* fail as a parent. So admit your failures faster. Seek forgiveness. Repent. And keep growing. That's what our kids need! Trust Jesus with eternity and with your parenting, and consider the power of His words:

> *My Father is glorified by this: that you produce much fruit and prove to be my disciples.*
> **JOHN 15:8**

> *Every tree that doesn't produce good fruit is cut down and thrown into the fire. So you'll recognize them by their fruit.*
> **MATTHEW 7:19-20**

If John is right, and there really is "no greater joy" than to hear of those "walking in truth" (3 John 4), then what are we waiting for?

This week in your group time and in your weekly parenting guide, we're going to lay the groundwork for studying the fruit of the Spirit. We'll cover five points:

1. We must be spiritually connected.
2. The fruit of the Spirit is interconnected.
3. Growth takes time.
4. Growth begins in the home.
5. Growth continues in community.

Day 1
We Must Be Spiritually Connected.

If you worry you don't have what it takes to cultivate your kids in the fruit of the Spirit, you're in good company. The only way any parent can do this is by remaining in Jesus and being spiritually connected. Apart from Him, you can do nothing.

Consider what Jesus said,

> *Truly I tell you, unless a grain of wheat falls to the ground and dies, it remains by itself. But if it dies, it produces much fruit.*
> **JOHN 12:24**

To grow in the fruit of the Spirit means we crucify our flesh and surrender our lives to Jesus Christ. From that moment of salvation, "the Spirit of God lives in you" (1 Cor. 3:16). But what does that mean for our kids, especially if they developmentally aren't yet able to understand what it means to receive Jesus as their Savior and Lord?

We believe kids understand more than we think. The environment we establish in our homes is critical for the seed of salvation to give birth to life in our kids. We want our homes to be permeated with the gospel.

Let's consider the moment Jesus rebuked the disciples when parents were taking their children to Jesus.

> *People were bringing little children to him in order that he might touch them, but the disciples rebuked them. When Jesus saw it, he was indignant and said to them, "Let the little children come to me. Don't stop them, because the kingdom of God belongs to such as these. Truly I tell you, whoever does not receive the kingdom of God like a little child will never enter it." After taking them in his arms, he laid his hands on them and blessed them.*
> **MARK 10:13-16**

Notice "the kingdom of God belongs to such as these" and "whoever does not receive the kingdom of God like a little child will never enter it." In other words, we must come to the gospel with a childlike faith.

Our kids are the perfect examples for us to learn how to trust Him!

Consider the soil (or the spiritual and emotional climate) of your home. Is it such that when your children hear the Word, they understand it experientially because they see it lived out as part of an everyday conversation?

> **Read Matthew 13:3-9,18-23. How does thinking of your own home being an environment where seeds are dropped for your children change how you read this passage?**

The Holy Spirit is the third Person of the holy Trinity—the Father, the Son, and the Holy Spirit. He is indeed a Person, not some spiritual force.

Read Jesus' words:

> *But the Counselor, the Holy Spirit, whom the Father will send in my name, will teach you all things and remind you of everything I have told you.*
> **JOHN 14:26**

What role does the Holy Spirit currently play in your life?

Read the following verses. Make a list of what you learn about the Holy Spirit.

Romans 8:1-11

Romans 8:26-27

Ephesians 4:30

2 Thessalonians 2:13-14

Accurate or inaccurate, what beliefs about the Holy Spirit do you carry into this study?

What has prevented you from pursuing the Holy Spirit in a deeper, more intimate way?

Read Luke 17:33; Galatians 5:24-25; and Philippians 1:21. In one sentence, write down your greatest takeaway from these passages about being spiritually connected.

PARENT GUIDE

In what ways do your children see you dying to self?

In what ways do you see your kids growing close to God? (Asking to pray, reading the Bible, choosing to obey, singing Bible songs, etc.)

If you were to ask your kids who Jesus is to them, what do you think they would say?

M(
Fa
I p
rig

DI
Te

BE
Te

AC
Th
so
so
ga

Th
wh
wi
of
th
we

Application

MORNING PRAYER
Lord, I pray my kids receive salvation in Jesus Christ. May my children come to know, love, and serve You all the days of their lives.

DINNERTIME STORY
Tell each of your children one fruit of the Spirit you see them living out and you admire.

BEDTIME QUESTION
What values do you think God wants to see in us?

ACTIVITY
Sit down around the table together tonight as a family. Ask your kids make a list of five things they admire about each of their siblings. Talk about them as a family. Go around the table and honor each child aloud. Use construction paper, markers, crayons, or other creative ways to make these lists. Encourage your kids post their honor lists where your family can see them. Help your children, one time each day, practice using the list to find a creative way to honor their brother(s) or sister(s). Parents, you too! Write an honor list for your spouse while the kids work on theirs.

Day 4
Growth Begins in the Home.

As far back as the Old Testament, Moses implored families to repeat the words of God to their children—to "talk about them when you sit in your house and when you walk along the road, when you lie down and when you get up" (Deut. 6:7).

If your children are little fruit trees, then consider your home the orchard.

Paul later wrote in the New Testament,

> *Fathers, don't stir up anger in your children, but bring them up in the training and instruction of the Lord.*
> **EPHESIANS 6:4**

The Greek word for "training" in this verse means *to counsel,* and refers to placing the mind in a proper place, as to reason with our kids by "warning [or] admonition."[1]

Eugene Peterson's paraphrase of this verse beautifully illustrates this principle:

> *Fathers, don't exasperate your children by coming down hard on them. Take them by the hand and lead them in the way of the Master.*
> **EPHESIANS 6:4, THE MESSAGE**

This is where we see a clear distinction between raising our kids with natural character traits and cultivating the supernatural fruit of the Spirit.

Raising our kids with character traits is not a bad thing. Yet in the natural world, one character trait at the expense of another can be challenging. For example, teaching our kids to be nice to others is noble. But if our kids become nice because they're afraid of rejection, the character trait is built on selfish motives. Instead, when we teach our kids that kindness means we look out for the best interests of others, we can cultivate the supernatural work of the Spirit in our kids to *faithfully* confront their friends for

wrong behavior in a *gentle, kind,* and *loving* way, *patiently* waiting for the "right time and procedure" (Eccl. 8:6).

Granted, this happens when we as parents, "remain in" the vine ourselves (John 15:4-5) and lead our kids "in the way of the Master" (Eph. 6:4, The Message).

To emphasize this point, one research study set out to find the top ten parenting strategies that achieve the outcomes we're looking for in our kids.[2] As you may guess—and consistent with remaining in the vine—love and affection came in at the top of the list. But what shocked even the researcher is that the second greatest parenting strategy to get the outcomes we're looking for in our kids is how a parent manages his or her own stress.

As sociologist Brené Brown writes, "The question isn't so much 'Are you parenting the right way?' as it is: 'Are you the adult that you want your child to grow up to be?'"[3]

How does it make you feel as a parent when your child doesn't want to read the Bible or pray?

How have you viewed your role as being a discipler to your child?

In what specific ways do you see yourself discipling your child?

As parents, we will mess up. We will say things we regret. We will yell. We will be inconsistent. However, as Romans 8 confirms, beating ourselves up for it does no good.

 # Bonus Application

MORNING PRAYER

Heavenly Father, surround my children with friends, mentors, and loved ones who champion and affirm our family values.

DINNERTIME STORY

Talk to your children about your favorite teacher or coach in school. Describe what made him or her your favorite and the values he or she instilled in you.

BEDTIME QUESTION

When did you feel most proud of yourself today or this week?

ACTIVITY

Buy some seeds for a garden. If you don't have a garden, plant some flowers in your home. To further illustrate the point, you could also plant a fruit tree in your yard, depending on where you live.

Use the beginning of this study to plant some roots. In other words, allow the tree to be a marker of your growing family over time. Whether you plant something small in the garden or as large as a tree in the yard, explain botanical growth to your children. The deeper the roots, the stronger the foundation and the more adversity the tree can withstand (Ps. 1:3). The shallower the root system, the less it can weather.

Ask your children to join you in planting the seed and watering it each day. Keep a journal with them of what they are doing each week to help the plant or tree grow. How much water does it need? Sunlight? Shade? Did you need to skip a day because it rained? Then, teach them to monitor the growth and journal its progress over time.

Use this plant or tree as an ongoing illustration in your home of their spiritual growth and the irrigation system necessary for producing fruit.

understanding My Child

Understanding each child individually helps us know how we can best teach biblical principles. Just as some plants need a lot of water to survive, and other plants need very little water, our kids grow differently. We want our kids to be interested in what they learn. If learning the Bible is boring for them, it won't be pleasant for anyone. Keep it fun!

For example, make a list below of each of your children's names. Beside each name, write down the best way you could help that particular child memorize the sixty-six books of the Bible. By having him or her:

- Repetitively write the books in order.
- Write a song or rap about the books of the Bible and record a music video together.
- Create a game or puzzle. Use markers to write all sixty-six books creatively on construction paper, cutting them out, and then placing them in order.
- Find a song online that recites the sixty-six Bible books and listen to it before bed or during drive time.

If you're studying with a group, take some time to discuss a few of the concepts from last week's personal and family study. What worked for you? What kinds of questions did your kids ask? We'll provide some discussion points and questions each week on these pages to help guide your conversation.

1. We Must Be Spiritually Connected.

As a group, read Galatians 5:22-24 aloud.

Spiritual connection begins with salvation. As we use the analogy of being homegrown throughout the study, think about a seed. Farmers and gardeners alike know that in order for a seed to produce fruit, first it must die.

How does this concept relate to our salvation and our spiritual lives?

Read John 14:26. What role does the Holy Spirit currently play in your life? In the life of your family?

Read Jesus' words in John 15:4-5 aloud.

What does it mean to "remain in" Jesus?

No matter the age of your children, how can you introduce them to Jesus? What word pictures can you use? How can you describe salvation?

2. The Fruit of the Spirit Are Interconnected.

Take notice of the word "fruit" in Galatians 5:22 and how it's singular. The list that follows is plural predicate, meaning they all go together.

If you feel comfortable, share with the group which fruit of the Spirit God has cultivated in you the strongest and which need more cultivation.

What about your kids? Which do you see in their lives and which need to be cultivated more?

3. Growth Takes Time.

What are some ways you can stay encouraged as a parent, even during a spiritual "drought"?

Read Psalm 1:1-3 aloud.

Verse 3 describes what's needed for the tree to grow: "flowing streams," or irrigation systems. With this analogy in mind, what irrigation systems do your children need over time to produce fruit?

4. Growth Begins in the Home.

Read Deuteronomy 6:7. Since God established the family as the breeding ground for spiritual growth, what are some ways you can make your home more healthy and hospitable for growth?

How do you feel when you think about being a discipler to your children? What has held you back in stepping into the role of discipler to your children?

How does Romans 8:1-2 affect your mind-set as a parent?

5. Growth Continues in Community.

Though growth begins in the home, it continues in community. Paul wrote, "Do not be deceived: 'Bad company corrupts good morals'" (1 Cor. 15:33). On the positive side, "Iron sharpens iron, and one person sharpens another" (Prov. 27:17).

With whom do you surround yourself? Can you "recognize them by their fruit" (Matt. 7:16)?

What about the people who surround your kids? Are they growing in a spiritually and emotionally safe environment that challenges their growth but gives them the support they need?[8]

RESTORE THE JOY OF YOUR

salvation

TO ME, AND

sustain

ME BY GIVING ME A

willing spirit.

PSALM 51:12

SESSION 2: LOVE + JOY

I (Josh) remember having a desire to know what it meant to be a man of character. I grew up, not just in a family of divorce, but also in a community of divorce. It was everywhere. I saw adulterous affairs, cheating, and manipulation of others' relationships, even in the church. I didn't want to be defined by any of this.

So, in my early twenties, I did a Bible word search on *character* and it led me to what is now one of my favorite passages of Scripture: Romans 5:1-5. Paul wrote, "… we rejoice in the hope of the glory of God. And not only that, but we also rejoice in our afflictions …" (vv. 2b-3a). Rejoice in affliction? But why? He then said, "… because we know that affliction produces endurance, endurance produces proven character, and proven character produces hope" (vv. 3b-4).

When I first read this I thought it was a bum deal. I would ask God, *You mean I have to suffer to get character?* Now, the older I get, the more I realize it's because of these strong storms that I grew stronger roots in Christ. But in those storms, I had my parents walk alongside me. I had mentors who sat with me in the pain. One mentor continues to tell me to this day when I call him in affliction, "Josh, let's celebrate this. What wisdom can you harvest from it?"

That's the difference between the fruit of joy and happiness. Happiness is elusive because it's an emotion that requires circumstances be aligned just right in our lives. Joy, on the other hand, is not an emotion but a state of being—not based on circumstances but on who we are in Christ. And the secret to experiencing that deep joy, even in the strongest storms of life, is found in the love of Christ for us.

It's no coincidence that the fruit of the Spirit begins with love. Look at the greatest commandment: "Love the Lord your God with all your heart, with all your soul, and with all your mind" (Matt. 22:37). What's the second greatest commandment? "Love your neighbor as yourself" (v. 39). But how do we love God, our neighbor, or even ourselves? It's found also in the secret to experiencing true joy: "We love because he first loved us" (1 John 4:19).

As we teach our kids about love and joy, keep in mind that joy comes from the Holy Spirit through our faith in Jesus Christ and is refined in suffering (Rom. 5:3-5; Jas. 1:2-4). True joy comes from placing our faith in the only secure, unshakable constant in our lives: the love of Jesus Christ for us (John 3:16; 1 John 3:16).

Day 1
What Is Love?

Do you know that "Sanskrit has ninety-six words for love; ancient Persian has eighty"?[1] Greek has four words, and English has only one. It's no wonder we confuse *love* in our American culture.

In the Greek language, *phileo* means "brotherly love"; *storge* means "love between family members"; *eros* is "romantic love"; and *agape* is "unconditional, godly love." The Bible uses each of these four words at different times. God's love for us, though, is unconditional.

We don't always feel God's *agape* love. Perhaps we don't feel it because what's most loving at the time is to protect us instead of giving us what we ask. To illustrate it with an earthly example, our kids might want candy, and because we say no, they don't feel like we love them. On the contrary, we deny them the candy because we do love them and don't want them to have too much sugar.

Read Deuteronomy 6:4-9 and 1 John 4:7–5:4.

What do these passages teach you about love?

What do you see as the relationship between fear, love, and faith?

Fear is the antithesis of faith. It also tends to hide love. What do you need from God to experience more of His love for you? What's one step you can take to increase your faith and decrease your fear?

 Application

MORNING PRAYER

Father, I pray today that my children will grow to love You with all of their hearts, minds, souls, and strength (Matt. 22:37).

DINNERTIME STORY

Talk about God's love. Tell your kids about the ways you know God loves you. Tell about a specific time you had a "Wow! God loves me!" moment.

BEDTIME QUESTION

How does God show you that He loves you?

ACTIVITY

The Love Seat: Take turns going around putting someone on the "love seat." The person on the "love seat" receives love from everyone else in the room. For instance, you might say to the person: *I love it when you _____ [make us a yummy dinner]; I love you because _____ [you make me laugh]; I especially like it when you _____ [play with me]; I appreciate you when _____ [you help unload the dishwasher].* You get the idea. Play so that every member of the family takes a turn on the "love seat."

Day 2
Experiencing God's Love

Read Psalm 103:8-10,13-14.

What does this passage say about God as our Father? Whom is He compassionate toward?

How do these verses speak to God's *agape* love?

Tell of an example in your life when you've experienced *agape* love from another person or shown *agape* love to someone.

Read Romans 8:35-39.

Take a few moments and reflect on this passage. Do you struggle, experientially, believing this passage of Scripture? Why or why not? Spend a few minutes in prayer asking God to show you His deep love for you.

Another type of love important to address with our children is *phileo*, or brotherly love. Proverbs 18:24 says,

> *One with many friends may be harmed, but there*
> *is a friend who stays closer than a brother.*
> **PROVERBS 18:24**

32   HOMEGROWN

Another passage reads,

> *Iron sharpens iron, and one person sharpens another.*
> **PROVERBS 27:17**

**Who is one of your friends "who stays closer than a brother"?
Do you talk to your kids about this friend?**

**What does the love of your friend mean to you? Give examples of
how you and your friend have been there for one another.**

This is a great way to model for our kids what true friends are all about. Our children learn from us in more ways than one. If they see healthy, spiritually nourishing relationships from us, they are more likely to look for those relationships themselves. Make an effort to talk about and with your friends in loving ways in front of your children. They'll learn that you value brotherly love through your example.

On the other hand, consider 1 Corinthians 15:33:

> *Do not be deceived: "Bad company corrupts good morals."*
> **1 CORINTHIANS 15:33**

**Can your kids identify the kids who are not a good influence on them?
What about the friends they know who love others well?**

Teach your children qualities to look for as well as
qualities to avoid in their friendships.

Application

MORNING PRAYER

Loving Father, please help my children learn to love their neighbors (Matt. 22:39).

DINNERTIME STORY

Tell your kids the greatest love story ever told—the story of how Jesus laid down His life for us. If you want to read it from a children's Bible or your personal Bible you can do that, but explain the story in detail. Help your kids see what Jesus did for them on the cross and why He chose to die for them. If your children are ready, lead them into placing their trust in Jesus' unconditional and sacrificial love for them.

BEDTIME QUESTION

Who has shown you love? How did they show you love?

ACTIVITY

Love God; Love Others: Take 3 x 5 inch index cards and write down ways you can show God's love to others by serving them. For example, you can write things like praying for a friend, helping with the dishes, being kind to my siblings, feeding those who are hungry, giving money or a gift to someone in need, writing a thank-you letter, visiting the elderly, holding the door for someone, giving someone a hug, raking a neighbor's leaves, and so forth. Invite your kids to come up with some ideas as well.

Pass the cards around and tell each person to take one card. That person will say aloud what they picked and give an idea of how they could carry out that act of love. See who can carry out their act of love by the end of the day. For extra fun, have a reward for those who were able to complete their act of love. Lead them to explain how they felt as a result of their actions.

Day 3
Loving Well

One of my closest friends, who is both gifted at and loves starting businesses, regularly discussed micro- and macroeconomics with his son growing up. As the loving father that he is, he uses business projects to train his son for the real world.

Recently, while on a year-long mission trip to Costa Rica as a family, he decided to help his son, who was sixteen at the time, earn money with a microfinancing project using an incredible woodworker in a local village. Not only would this project teach his son how to earn money, it would help the woodworker and the local economy as well.

As he told me about it, I could hear in his voice the excitement for his son. The further involved they got, the more passionate my friend became.

About a week later, my friend called me sounding unusually depressed. He said, "Josh, you know this project we've been working on? Well, my son looked at me and said, 'Dad, this is your project with my name on it. If you want me to learn, let me do something that I'm passionate about.'"

I asked my friend how he responded. He said they went for a walk along the beach, and after listening to his son's point of view, he looked at his son and said, "You know, you're right. I'm sorry."

My friend continued, "I asked him what he wanted to do. No rules applied. He told me he wanted to build a space hotel. So that's where we started."

What my friend realized was that even though his intentions were so incredibly good-willed, he actually did his son a disservice by overstepping his bounds and quarterbacking the project for him.

"I went from teaching him a lesson to letting him watch a lesson," he concluded. "I realized how imperfect my actions can be even though my intentions for my kids may be pure."

If you read the passage in 1 John 4, "perfect love drives out fear" (v. 18), and were left with the lingering thought in your mind, *All of this perfect love and "parenting without fear" stuff is great, but I'm not God,* that's right where you need to be.

If we try to be perfect, then we'll parent out of fear. If we think we should never make a mistake, we'll make parenting choices out of fear. If we ebb and flow with the latest parenting technique and strategy, choosing to give time-outs this week and not give them the next, we'll parent out of fear.

So let yourself off the hook now—you won't parent perfectly.

The opposite of love is not hate. The opposite of love is fear. To put it simply, an unsafe environment instills fear. A safe environment rids itself of fear.

Just think of the fearful ways we *react* to our kids in stressful moments when they act out. Yelling. Blaming. Punishing. Shaming. Maybe even spanking out of anger. When we *react* to our kids out of the insecurities from our own stories, we do so from fear—fear of our kids turning out a certain way, fear of treating our kids the way our parents treated us, fear of losing control as a parent, or perhaps even fear of being seen as a bad parent.[2]

> **What are the fears you carry that inhibit your ability to love well? Perfectionism? A parental agenda?**

> **What word best describes your current home environment: *fearful, loving, authoritative, permissive, busy*? Why did you choose that word?**

When we as parents react to our kids out of fear, it's not their misbehavior our kids are thinking about—it's the fear of disconnection they feel from the person who is supposed to be the emotionally safest in their lives.[3] This is how the tendency to recreate the cycle of fear is rooted in our own stories.[4]

What word in the previous question would your children use to best describe your current home environment?

What one step will you take to move more toward an environment of love this week?

Choosing to be an imperfect parent is choosing to be a loving parent. So feel free to mess up—but be quick to work to repair the relationship. Scripture calls this forgiveness and tells us to practice it a lot.

By repairing a rupture in our relationship with our kids, we free them from any expectation to be perfect themselves. Not only that, it teaches our kids the appropriate way of handling imperfection when they make a mistake as well.

Simply using the words "I'm sorry. Will you forgive me?" as they relate to a specific offense with your kids and then changing your behavior toward them speaks more about who you are than anything else you do. Owning your imperfection makes you emotionally safer and more loving than trying to be perfect.

Perfect love requires that we own up to our imperfections.

What's easy or difficult about saying "I'm sorry. Will you forgive me?" to your kids?

The difference between guilt and shame when loving our kids is important. Guilt is healthy and means, "I made a mistake." Shame is unhealthy and means, "I am a mistake."

Which do you find yourself carrying more of as a parent?

Where do you most struggle when it comes to cultivating an environment of love for your kids?

How do your kids most receive love from you? Keep in mind, this is likely different for each child.

How do each of your children express love?

The Bible says,

> *Don't neglect to show hospitality, for by doing this some have welcomed angels as guests without knowing it.*
> **HEBREWS 13:2**

Do you have a story about a time you may have welcomed an angel as a guest without knowing it by how you loved someone? Describe it here. Make a note to share it with your kids this week.

Sometimes, on earth, love doesn't work out. Josh's parents divorced when he was ten. If you have broken marriages in your family lineage, or you're a part of a blended family or are a single parent today because of divorce, use this as an opportunity to explain—respectfully—that because of the fall of man, romantic love doesn't always work out here on earth. However, that doesn't mean that God doesn't love us or will divorce us (Rom. 8:35-39).

If you have a personal story you can tell—age-appropriately—about how God redeemed brokenness in your family and showed His unconditional love through the pain, tell it to your kids. Kids see that love on earth doesn't always work out. This is our chance to help them see how God never leaves us or abandons us (Deut. 31:6).

# Application

MORNING PRAYER

Father, I pray my children become firmly planted in love and joy.

DINNERTIME STORY

Tell your kids about a moment you felt proud of them for showing a joyful spirit, especially during difficult circumstances (e.g., it rained on a planned day at the amusement park, etc.).

BEDTIME QUESTION

Who or what brought you the most joy today?

ACTIVITY

I've Got the Joy: You may know the song, "I've Got the Joy," by George W. Cooke. Teach and sing this song with your kids. The modernized verse we laugh at as a family is: "And if the devil doesn't like it, he can sit on a tack (ouch)." If you're unfamiliar with the song, find a video online to watch and learn with your kids.

If you have older kids, talk about songs you know that express joy. You could even make it a game, taking turns trying to think of songs with the word "joy" in the lyrics.

Use the song to teach your kids about the love and joy of Jesus. Ask questions like:

- What happened today that gave you the joy of Jesus?
- Did someone do something for you?
- Was someone kind to you?

Depending on the age of your children, you could even go a step further and ask if they were discouraged today—or if they got angry, sad, scared, or jealous. In other words, ask how the enemy tried to steal their joy today (John 10:10).

This activity is a great way to create conversation about how the devil can steal our joy and how to prevent that from happening. Close the activity by giving those frustrations to God in prayer, and then sing the song as loudly as you can as a family.

Day 4
What Is Joy?

There are grandmas, gigis, grannies, grandmommies, and nanas, and then there are memaws. I (Josh) had Memaw.

As a boy, I went to her house often. Sundays after church were special because my family got together and turned the peaceful ambiance of Memaw's home into playful chaos. My sister and I wrestled and nitpicked. Dad and I whipped each other with wet towels we had used to dry the dishes. The real fun was seeing who would end up with the bright orange "Special $.99" sticker from the chip bag on his or her back. After lunch, we napped, played cards, or watched football.

Memaw personified love. She did anything to help my sister and me mature into respectable adults. We spent many nights over at her house cooking, creating, and playing with homemade toys, and romping in the huge sandpiles situated at the block company next door to her home. She taught me that having little was just enough.

Then she was diagnosed with cancer.

As a graduate student in my early twenties, I lay beside Memaw crying the weekend before she died, planning her eulogy. I asked her, "Memaw, if there was one message you would like everyone to know, what would that be?" Through a groaning voice, writhing in pain, she responded, "Be joyful." Though I was quite shocked in the moment, it made sense. She was a woman who knew not to mourn as those "who have no hope" (1 Thess. 4:13). In that moment, Memaw showed me how God works in the midst of suffering.[5]

When you or your kids hit a difficult time, stop in that moment and ask God together to "fill you with all joy and peace as you believe" (Rom. 15:13). The reality is this: God is our only constant. In Him, we have all we need (Ps. 23:1). And because of Him we will all, as believers in Christ, one day rejoice with our loved ones.

Read the following verses. Write what each teaches you about joy.

Proverbs 17:22

Luke 2:10

Acts 2:46-47

James 1:2-4

3 John 4

How have you seen someone rejoice in the midst of suffering?

Why do you think it's important for your children and others to see you, as a believer, have joy no matter your circumstances?

 Application

MORNING PRAYER

Heavenly Father, instill in my children the joy of your salvation, and sustain them by giving them a willing spirit (Ps. 52:12).

DINNERTIME STORY

Time to pull out the dad jokes! What jokes did your parents tell you growing up? Use your time tonight at the dinner table to tell good, clean, and definitely corny jokes.

BEDTIME QUESTION

What is one way our family could be more joyful?

ACTIVITY

Make Me Laugh: This is just a fun game to play to get everyone in a giggly mood. Each person takes a turn. They can tell a joke, make a funny face, tell a funny story, or ask a ridiculous question. The goal is for that person to make others laugh. If you want to keep score, you can do so by seeing who made others laugh the fastest, who made the most people laugh at once, and you can also give a special prize to whoever completed the funniest act!

Day 5
Experiencing Joy

We went through a period early in our parenting journey that wasn't much fun. Our newborn baby screamed more than she slept, and Josh's dad went through three major heart surgeries. With two kids ages two and under and driving twenty-one hours to be with Josh's dad, we were barely functioning and rarely laughing.

So we did what anyone would do: We bought a picture of a cow. Learning about the importance of laughing for the first seven seconds of the day,[6] we hung this hilarious picture of a cow in our bedroom where we would see it and laugh upon waking.

Psalm 126 talks about laughter. After the Lord restored Zion, the psalmist says,

> *Our mouths were filled with laughter then, and our tongues*
> *with shouts of joy. Then they said among the nations,*
> *"The LORD has done great things for them." The LORD*
> *had done great things for us; we were joyful.*
> **PSALM 126:2-3**

Why were the people laughing in this passage?

How does our laughter display the glory of the Lord?

Laugh with your kids. I (Christi) don't know about you, but if I'm not intentional about it, my time spent with the kids can look more like nagging and telling them no, instead of laughing and celebrating the yes. If your kids ask you to do something, instead of immediately saying, "No," ask yourself, "Why not?" If you can't come up with a legitimate reason, let the memory unfold.

Put down what you're doing. The dishes will be there later. You can clean up the house with your spouse after the kids are in bed. Stop what you're doing and enter your kids' world of laughter. Tell jokes. Have a dance party. Get into a pillow fight. Draw funny pictures. See who can make the funniest sound, the craziest dance move, or imitate a television character, like Donald Duck®.

Practice turning your home into a laugh factory, to borrow a phrase from *Monsters, Inc.*, If we don't create room for our kids to laugh, they'll learn not to laugh.

What keeps you from laughing, from embracing joy in the mundane?

What are two ways you can create more laughter in your home?

As adults, we tend to suppress joy in our kids for various reasons. Getting our kids ready for bed one night, Christi took our daughter's soiled diaper (no, it wasn't a number two) and hit me in the head with it from across the room. It ended in the playroom with me covering my head in fear of it actually coming unwrapped. The laughter filled our house. For the next week, every night we tucked our kids into bed to discover their favorite part of the day was "when mommy hit you with the diaper."

The daily grind is real. But let's be honest—if we're not laughing, we're not living.

Many of us miss joy because we wait for something extraordinary to happen. However, one study looked at people who had experienced unfathomable loss.[7] Without exception, every participant mentioned the mundane moments they remembered most about their loved ones.

"If I could come downstairs and see my husband sitting at the table [with] the newspaper ..."[8]

"My mom sent me the craziest texts—She never knew how to work her phone. I'd give anything to get one of those texts right now."[9]

Even when you're frustrated, stressed, and tired, embrace the small moments. Your child's belly laugh. The way your spouse expresses excitement. Seeing your children embrace in a hug or look out for one another.

Picture yourself sitting around the dinner table twenty-five to thirty years from now with your kids' family, your grandchildren begging for stories. What you won't hear from your own kids is how well you kept the kitchen clean, how you successfully had them in bed by 7:30 p.m. every night, or how you taught them never to splash the water out of the bathtub.

Instead, you'll hear about Mom and Dad's diaper fight through the house, the time the whole family got caught in the rain out on a walk and decided to just dance, the time you stayed up past bedtime to play games as a family, the camping trip, the pancake dates, and the leaf piles in the fall.

If you're like us, you may be uptight about schedules, routines, not getting the kitchen messy from a food fight, or the kids getting sweaty again following a bath. We all have our areas where we need to let loose a bit.

What one activity or request of your child can you say yes to this week that will stretch you a bit?

Think back through the last week. Write down moments of joy you experienced, no matter how extraordinary or ordinary the moment. Practice this on an ongoing basis.

Start a routine where you find the joy in painful moments with your kids too. Maybe it's a low grade on a report card. A friend made fun of them at school. A grandparent becomes ill. Whatever the pain point, take your child on a one-on-one date together to talk about it. Go fishing. Go for pancakes. Do something you and your child love doing together and share together the wisdom you can harvest from the situation. When our kids learn to celebrate the painful moments, it sets them up for a life of problem-solving, character, and joy.

 Application

MORNING PRAYER

Father, today our family shouts "for joy because of the works of your hands" (Ps. 92:4).
Thank You for _____ [insert a specific way God has blessed your family with joy].

DINNERTIME STORY

Tell your kids the story of how you and your spouse met for the first time. Tell them funny stories or about any notable events from when you were dating or how you got engaged. Show your kids pictures or video of your wedding day.

BEDTIME QUESTION

If you could change one thing about the world, what would it be?

ACTIVITY

Love Notes: Encourage your family to let one another know how much you care all day long by sending each other love notes. Cut out a stack of hearts from pink, red, and white paper. Write little messages on the paper about how much you love them. Then, hide them in unexpected places. Put them in jacket pockets, in car seats, in computer bags, in shoes, in lunch boxes, in cereal bowls, under pillows, tucked into pajamas, or in books. Depending on the age of your kids, you'll likely need to help them write their messages for siblings.

 # Bonus Application

MORNING PRAYER

Holy Spirit, work in the hearts of my children and fill them with abundant joy (Gal. 5:22).

DINNERTIME STORY

Tell your kids about a difficult moment in your life and how you found joy in that moment. What did that trial teach you? How did you grow in character? Use this as a chance to teach what it means to "rejoice in our afflictions" (Rom. 5:3).

BEDTIME QUESTION

What are you struggling with the most right now (grades, activities, peers, at home, etc.)? How can I help?

ACTIVITY

Love Is … You can be as elaborate as you'd like with this activity. Ask your kids to make a display of 1 Corinthians 13 as a reminder of how we should show love to others.

You can find a piece of wood and create your own sign as a family, buy a small canvas at a craft store and let your kids paint their own picture, or you could help your kids create their own with a simple piece of construction paper.

Read through 1 Corinthians 13:4-7 with your kids around the table. Help them understand what it means to envy, keep a record of wrongs, and so forth. Encourage each person to read it with his or her name in the place of "love" in the passage (i.e. Ellie is patient; Cooper is kind, etc.). When you're done with everyone's names, put Jesus' name in there.

Use this as an ongoing reminder of what it means to "be the love of Jesus." Display the pictures in a place where you can keep the conversation going with your kids and continually teach them what love is.

Understanding My Child

Teaching our kids facts about the Bible early on is important because our children developmentally learn this way. As preschoolers, teaching them the books of the Bible, singing songs about it, and telling them stories from the Bible are great ways to start instilling in them knowledge of Scripture. Look for Bible songs online that teach the books of the Bible. Find a children's Bible storybook. Then, begin by using one of the four keys times of the day mentioned in the introduction to teach. For instance, your day could include any of the following.

- Sing songs full of Scripture as you get ready in the morning.
- Recite the books of the Bible, or practice Bible verse memorization while driving to the grocery store or school.
- Talk to your kids at dinnertime about your favorite Bible passages or how the Bible is impacting your own life right now.
- Tell Bible stories as you tuck your children into bed.

If you're studying with a group, take some time to discuss a few of the concepts from last week's personal and family study. What worked for you? What kinds of questions did your kids ask? We'll provide some discussion points and questions each week on these pages to help guide your conversation.

1. What Is Love?

As a group, read 1 Corinthians 13:4-7 aloud.

Which of the descriptions of love do you feel best characterizes you? Which areas do you know you need to grow in love?

Can you tell which characteristics of love you need to teach your children about most? Describe ways you can cultivate each of these in your kids in a practical way. Share ideas as a group.

2. Experiencing God's Love

Someone read 1 John 4:10-13,19 aloud.

Do you believe God loves you? Why or why not? Be honest about your experience with God's love for you.

How do you personally and practically experience God's love for you right now? What role does the Holy Spirit play in your experience of God's love?

Name a recent moment when you felt God's overwhelming love for you so strongly that you stopped and said, "Wow, God, You love me!"

How can you help your kids find those moments each day?

3. Loving Well

Someone read 1 John 4:16-18 aloud.

What are the fears you carry that inhibit your ability to love well? Perfectionism? A parental agenda?

What word best describes your current home environment: *fearful, loving, authoritative, permissive, busy*? Why did you choose that word?

What word in the question above would your children use to best describe your current home environment?

What one step will you take to move more toward an environment of love this week?

4. What Is Joy?

Someone read Psalm 51:12 aloud.

How have you experienced "the joy of your salvation"? What holds you back from experiencing joy in your life?

Read Romans 5:1-5 aloud.

What stands out to you about this passage?

What is the Holy Spirit's role in this passage?

5. Experiencing Joy

Someone read Jeremiah 31:1-5,12-13 aloud.

What's the people's response to God's redeeming love? What details stand out to you in this passage?

How does your child express joy? Talk about a moment when you looked on with awe because you saw joy in your child.

What can you do to keep cultivating a true expression of joy in your children?

I HAVE TOLD YOU THESE

things

SO THAT IN ME YOU MAY HAVE

peace.

YOU WILL HAVE SUFFERING IN THIS WORLD.

Be courageous!

I HAVE CONQUERED

the world.

JOHN 16:33

SESSION 3: PEACE + PATIENCE

Patience is likely to be the most bitter-tasting fruit we address. When we recently polled more than 700 families of their top parenting struggle, we found "losing my patience" to be in the top four! Yet, how often do you find yourself praying for patience? Rarely or never, right? *If I pray for patience,* the thought goes, *then God is going to put me through a trial to test it.* And since we don't need any more difficulties, we avoid the topic of patience altogether.

When we suffer, have to wait, or feel rejected, we get angry or upset that our lives just don't match up to what we expected or hoped for. This is especially true when we feel stuck in the survival years with screaming, sleepless kids and the harsh realization that being a parent isn't quite all we expected it to be.

In fact, the parenting journey can sometimes feel like Matthew 8:23-27, when the disciples cried out for their lives while waves swamped their boat. Think about the waves crashing into your boat—colicky babies, unruly kids, little sleep, exhaustion, discipline, health issues, and the stress it all has on your marriage. Like the disciples, however, we need to remember who is in the boat with us. We may not have any control over the winds and waves, but He does. And our trust in Him is where our peace is found. As Jesus said,

> *I have told you these things so that in me you may have peace. You will have suffering in this world. Be courageous! I have conquered the world.*
> **JOHN 16:33**

Being patient and living at peace requires trusting Jesus, even if it feels like He's sleeping during our trials. Cultivating patience and peace in our kids is a process that includes living with:

- A grateful heart
- A whole heart
- A present mind
- A patient attitude
- Eternity in mind

As you go through this session, think about how easy it is to lose your own patience or not feel at peace with your current circumstances. As always, let's begin there, and then put into practice what we ask of our kids.

Day 1
Living with a Grateful Heart

What first comes to your mind when you hear the word *peace*? Today we take selfies while holding up the universal two-finger gesture for peace, which originated in 1958 by Gerald Holtom for the British Campaign for Nuclear Disarmament. In fact, this anti-nuclear organization has often been at the forefront for peace in the UK and around the world.[1]

In spite of the genuine and heartfelt desire for no war, the peace that comes from the fruit of the Spirit doesn't come from without; it comes from within. To picture biblical peace, go back to the image of Jesus sleeping in the boat during the storm in Matthew 8:23-27, with the waves swamping the boat and the disciples crying out for their lives.

If only we could find a way to trust Him more.

Actually, we can. And it's a bit simpler than one might think. But it takes discipline and gratitude.

Yes, to have more peace in your life, just add some gratitude. In other words, focus your mind on how God already comes through for you each and every day.

Make a list of five things for which you're grateful.

1.

2.

3.

4.

5.

Ask your kids to do this exercise too. What are they grateful for? Have them do this exercise regularly. Being transformed by "the renewing of your mind" takes discipline (Rom. 12:2). To maintain a grateful heart takes time and practice.

In the Old Testament Hebrew, the word for peace is *shalom*, and it means, "'well-being and health, to be well, content and in a friendly state.' ... Furthermore, *shalom* is taken from the root word *shalam*, which means 'to be safe in mind, body, or estate.' It speaks of completeness, fullness, or a type of wholeness that encourages you to give back—to generously repay something in some way."[2] In addition, the New Testament Greek word is *eirene*, and means "joining what had previously been separated or disturbed," and signifies "setting at one; quietness; and rest."[3]

> **Considering the Greek definition of *peace*, is there a situation in your life that feels "separated or disturbed"? Perhaps it's a relationship marked by unforgiveness or a job you feel stuck in. A lack of peace can also come when your children get sick or are picked on at school.**

Oftentimes, a deep sense of fear is what prevents us from "setting at one" or being at rest. We don't feel peace because we're not "safe in mind, body, or estate."

> **What do you do when you're feeling anxious? Is there someone you call? Do you just want to sleep? Write down your initial reaction when you're feeling anxious about something.**

> **How can you tell when your child is anxious?**

> **Do you find that your fear response is different in varying situations (i.e. sick kids, financial pressure, family relationships, etc.)?**

In what situations do you find you trust God more easily? In what situations do you struggle most with trusting God? Our trust in God is usually lesser in situations of our strongest fear response.

Gratitude is nutrient rich soil. When storms—no matter how big or small—threaten to destroy the crop, people who harvest the fruit of peace turn to their Father in heaven. But the prayer begins with thanks to God—both for all He has done and for all He will do, even in the storm.

Peaceful people have learned to look back on their lives for how God has come through for them in the past—never leaving them or forsaking them.

Write down three ways God has shown you that you can trust Him.

1.

2.

3.

Let your kids do the previous exercise as well.

Read Matthew 6:25-34. What one thing jumps out to you personally about Jesus' words?

Using Matthew 6:25-34, write a note to yourself from Jesus. What do you need to be reminded of? Put this note on your bathroom mirror or car dash where you will see it on a regular basis.

Peaceful people have learned to thank God for how He is going to come through for them in the future, even if it's not the way they want it to be. In other words, they cling to Matthew 6:25-34 in a personal way and know hindsight is always 20/20.

Think of a situation you currently feel anxious about. What do you want to thank God for today that hasn't happened yet with that situation?

Begin the practice of developing peace by having each person in your family, kids included, start a gratitude journal. Buy something they will enjoy using. Add to it daily. Read it daily. And when you or your child's mind begins to worry, go to God in gratitude and ask Him for the peace that "surpasses all understanding" (Phil. 4:7).

 Application

MORNING PRAYER
Father, fill my kids' hearts and minds with Your peace when they're anxious (Phil. 4:7).

DINNERTIME STORY
What moments brought you peace as a kid? Share with your children moments that you look back on with a sense of peace. Did you share a room with your siblings? Was it playing a sport, instrument, or board games as a family? Was it Sunday afternoons at grandma's? Describe specific childhood moments for which you are grateful.

BEDTIME QUESTION
When do you feel most at peace?

ACTIVITY
Gratitude Scavenger Hunt: Being thankful increases our peace and helps us be more patient as we wait on the Lord. Developed originally as a game of gathering photos, this adapted version is used to increase our gratitude and verbally declare how God is working in our lives.

We have included a list below to help you get started, but feel free to add more prompts. You can do this during your drive time or at home. Go through the list,

and as your kids see sights, hear sounds, or think of something that comes to mind, allow them to state what they are grateful for, and check it off the list. You may also find it easier simply to go through the list together as a family. For an added keepsake, write down what your kids are thankful for now with the date and save it.[4]

Something I'm grateful for ...

☐ **Outside in the wilderness**

☐ **That makes a beautiful sound**

☐ **That tastes good**

☐ **That smells amazing**

☐ **That has been hard for me**

☐ **That I would like to share with others**

☐ **That's older than me**

☐ **That I recently discovered or learned**

☐ **That shows a lot of color**

☐ **That has words on it**

☐ **That makes me feel strong**

☐ **That makes me laugh**

☐ **That makes me cry**

☐ **Someone who plays with me**

☐ **Someone I love (outside of my family)**

☐ _____

☐ _____

☐ _____

☐ _____

☐ _____

Day 2
Living with a Whole Heart

As a mom, I (Christi) feel like I'm scattered a lot. The idea of "joining what had previously been separated or disturbed,"[5] feels impossible to me. I've been known to put my phone in the refrigerator and put the milk back in the pantry. I often wondered how to peacefully join my inner world when I can't seem to keep things together in my outer world.

Until one day I came across what has become one of my favorite stories about peace. Kay Arthur tells about a man named Jim Walton who was translating the New Testament for the Muinane people of La Sabana in the Columbian jungles. He couldn't figure out how to translate the biblical word for *peace*, until one day when he encountered Fernando, the village chief. Here's the story:

> Fernando, the village chief, was promised a 20-minute plane ride to a location that would have taken him 3 days to travel by walking. The plane was delayed in arriving at La Sabana, so Fernando departed on foot. When the plane finally came, a runner took off to bring Fernando back. But by the time he had returned, the plane had left. Fernando was livid because of the mix-up. He went to Jim and launched into an angry tirade. Fortunately, Walton had taped the chief's diatribe. When he later translated it, he discovered that the chief kept repeating the phrase, "I don't have one heart." Jim asked other villagers what having "one heart" meant, and he found that it was like saying, "There is nothing between you and the other person." That, Walton realized, was just what he needed to translate the word *peace*. To have *peace* with God means that there is nothing—no sin, no guilt, no condemnation—that separates us. And that *peace* with God is possible only through Christ (Rom. 5:1).[6]

We'll make mistakes. We'll put the milk in the pantry. We'll even yell at our kids. But no matter the circumstances, we can always pursue "one heart" with Jesus. For me, this looks like prayer time every morning before the kids are out of bed. I need this time, because when I'm not spending time with the Prince of peace, my heart gets scattered and I begin focusing on the impending storm. I'm less patient with my kids and not as kind or gentle with Josh.

Read Isaiah 9:6 and Luke 2:8-14.

How has Jesus been the Prince of peace for you?

How do you celebrate the coming of the Prince of peace with your kids at Christmastime? What's one way you can celebrate differently to focus on the fruit of peace?

Read Romans 5:1. What's currently separated or disturbed in your relationship with Jesus right now? Is there unrepentant sin? Unforgiveness? Even bitterness for how a situation didn't turn out?

Like the village chief said, what does it look like to have "one heart" with Jesus? How does having "one heart" affect your day-to-day life?

What's one spiritual discipline you can practice that will keep you in "one heart" with the Prince of peace?

 # Application

MORNING PRAYER

God, help me to have peace in You, so that I may model for my kids how to have peace in You.

DINNERTIME STORY

Tonight is kids' story time! Ask your kids to share stories. They can be fictional or true stories about what's going on in their lives. Give them a chance to share anything they desire. Be patient in their storytelling.

BEDTIME QUESTION

What do you want to thank God for tonight?

ACTIVITY

Direct your kids to draw a picture of a moment they recently felt scared, alone, or otherwise not at peace. When they're finished drawing the picture, let them talk about that moment with you. After they talk about it, ask them to draw Jesus in the picture beside them.

Now let them talk about what they see and how it would change the way they feel if they pictured Jesus with them when they felt scared or alone in the future. Depending on the age of your child, decorate the picture with a verse (Isa. 9:6; John 16:33) or simply write *Peace* across the top of the picture and hang it on the refrigerator as a reminder that Jesus is our Prince of peace.

Day 3
Living with a Present Mind

Many days we're tempted to think about work, our to-do list, or even finances when we're with our spouses or kids. But the moments that truly matter are those when our kids' hearts and minds are disturbed or overwhelmed.

How can you be more emotionally present for your kids when they are overwhelmed or anxious?

Here's a tip that's helped us in the past: If thoughts of the day tend to distract you when you're at home, find a healthy way to decompress before entering your children's presence. Work out. Go for a walk. Do something active. It may take more time, but it will set you up for success to be more fully engaged with those you love and are cultivating.

Read Ephesians 6:4.

> *Fathers, don't stir up anger in your children, but bring them up in the training and instruction of the Lord.*
> **EPHESIANS 6:4**

The Greek words for "training" and "instruction" literally means, "'a putting in mind,' then warning, admonition, instruction" so as to think about the right way of God.[7] When our kids are overwhelmed, throwing a tantrum, or otherwise not at peace, we, as parents, can be a finite peace that literally calms our child's brain so they can think straight again, not be overwhelmed by emotion, and choose the right way of God. As parents, we have the power to either provoke and disturb, or promote peace and unite our child's heart and mind. Your whole presence is crucial in these overwhelming moments.

How have you helped unite your child's inner turmoil and bring peace to his or her heart and mind in anxious situations?

In what ways have you provoked anger in your child previously?

Who was a coach, teacher, pastor, or boss you had who seemed to live in peace? How did he or she teach this lesson to you?

Another way to cultivate a present mind is to practice speaking peace in your home.

Read Genesis 3:20.

The man named his wife Eve because she was the mother of all the living.
GENESIS 3:20

The power of words starts in the beginning. Adam had the power to name his wife even after the fall. Instead of naming her "nag" or "exhausting" or even "worrywart," he named her "life." Eve.

Read the following verses and write down what each one teaches about the tongue or our words:

Psalm 12:4

Psalm 39:1

Psalm 139:4

Proverbs 15:4

Proverbs 31:26

How can you use your tongue to better cultivate peace and practice being truly present in your home?

What words does your spouse need from you? What words do your kids need?

What are some words, phrases, or tone of voice you're using now that your kids have picked up on? Write down some phrases you want to incorporate more into your everyday life with your kids.

As families, we go through a lot of suffering. Sometimes it's with our spouse. Quite often it's because of outside pressures like finances, work, or in-laws. But remember, you're a team. You're for one another, not against one another. We often need to remind ourselves of that.

 # Application

MORNING PRAYER

Lord, teach my children not to "worry about tomorrow" but to rely on You for what they need today (Matt. 6:34).

DINNERTIME STORY

Tell your children about one practical way you manage your fears and find peace with God—especially when you're immediately overwhelmed, caught off-guard, or facing danger of some kind.

BEDTIME QUESTION

When you get scared, what are ways you calm yourself down?

ACTIVITY

God's Got It: When we worry, it certainly doesn't feel like "God's got it." This is an activity that helps our children learn to relax, and even begin giving their fears to God from an early age. The idea behind this activity is for our kids to learn this one truth, that they can find peace within, because God's got it.

You know your children. Sometimes, you can easily sense when something is worrying them. Simply begin by asking your kids to name one thing they're afraid of. You could ask this question in a number of ways depending on the ages and maturity levels of your children: "What's one thing you're not looking forward to this week?" "Is there an event or situation coming up that you're anxious about?" You could even break the ice by simply beginning the discussion:

1. Tell your child to specifically verbalize his or her fear. (This alone reduces anxiety.)
2. Everybody, together, closes their eyes and takes slow, deep breaths.
3. Together recite Psalm 56:3—"When I am afraid, I will trust in you." Challenge your kids (and yourself) to memorize this verse to combat fearful lies with God's truth.
4. After reciting the verse, pray together, thanking God for being trustworthy and asking Him to help you trust Him in the midst of fear and worry.

Day 4
Living with a Patient Attitude

The other night our kids wanted a treat after dinner. Instead of immediately having dessert, we told them they had to earn it. If we had to clean up dinner, they had to help. Our son vacuumed the floor. Our daughter wiped the table and countertops. When the kitchen was cleaned, we all sat down together as a family to enjoy a treat.

Too often, we act as if our kids cannot do things themselves. Perhaps it's because we live such busy lives that it can seem easier just to do things for our kids instead of empowering them to independence. However, kids love structure. They need purpose. And quite often, they are more capable of doing hard things than we give them credit for. So to build patience in your kids, help them learn to do hard things first. But also treat them as if they can control themselves, because they can.

Teaching them constructive ways to wait—like singing a song, dancing in the mirror, or drawing a picture—fosters patience. Also, instead of immediately jumping to their requests—like getting a napkin at dinner—put the napkins in a place where they can get them on their own.

Finally, show them their limits. If your toddler is pulling food out of the pantry, gently put the items back and teach her the limits. If she's throwing food on the floor, pick it up and put in back on the plate while she's present. A child who learns to get away with what she wants is a child who learns to rule the house.

Read or skim the Book of Jonah (don't worry; it's a short book).

Was God more patient with Jonah or Nineveh?

Read Jonah 4:4. What does this teach you about your response to God when things aren't going the way you want?

How can you lovingly translate this verse to your kids when they don't get their way?

Waiting can be a daunting task. Too often we get so self-focused on waiting for what we want that we miss what we really need. Imagine what the Israelites had to go through—being led out of Egypt in great anticipation for the promised land—only to be held in the desert for forty years.

Or worse yet, imagine the time God's people waited for the coming Messiah—more than 400 years after Isaiah prophesied that God would send the Prince of peace into the world as a sacrifice for our sins. Four hundred years of desperate silence.

And we think waiting on slow Internet is brutal!

Too often we wait with the wrong attitude. It can leave us bitter and overly focused on what we want, perhaps not what's best for us. The longer we wait with such an attitude, the more likely we are to lose hope that what we're waiting on will ever happen.

Cultivating patient kids takes time. Teaching them to play on their own (and not with a screen) and helping them find their own interests are two ways to build patience. When we find things we love doing, time passes by.

In an *In This Together* podcast episode, we interviewed Dr. John Townsend, a best-selling author and psychologist. We asked him how to raise our kids not to be entitled. One of his responses was to teach them to "do hard things first."[8] Proverbs 16:32 says, "Patience is better than power, and controlling one's emotions, than capturing a city."

What hard thing did you do at an early age that helped you develop patience?

What hard thing can you encourage your children through?

When we show our kids that they have what it takes to do hard things, we empower them to be patient. If we tie our kids' shoes all of the time, they won't learn how to do it themselves. If we rescue them from consequences, they'll stay in the same behavior.

Likewise, if our kids see us being impatient, it will foster the same characteristic in them.

How have you been impatient with your kids?

What attitude has contributed to your impatience (e.g. expecting your kids to learn the first time, time constraints, demands, etc.)?

Read 1 Samuel 1:1-20.

What do you learn from Hannah's waiting?

***Waiting* is a verb, not a noun. Like Hannah, what are ways you can learn to be active in your waiting?**

How can you teach your kids to be active in their waiting?

Read the words of David, a man familiar with waiting:

> *I waited patiently for the LORD, and he turned to me and heard my cry for help.*
> **PSALM 40:1**

Sometimes we give up in our active waiting because we lose patience and don't think God is going to come through.

What do you need to increase your faith in God's provision for your life?

To cultivate patience and fight instant gratification, think about what you turn to when you're finally alone. When the kids are down for the night, or you finally have a minute together as a couple, what's the first thing you do? (Clean the house? Browse Instagram®? Turn on a favorite show?)

Practice putting off "checking out." If you can get this practice down, you'll be able to much more easily pass it onto your kids.

Choose projects and activities that require connecting with time and patience, such as baking, rearranging furniture in the house, or even sitting down to slower-moving games like Scrabble®, checkers, or Monopoly®. Do all of these without the phone.

Another helpful activity that requires patience is setting up an emergency fund or saving money for a vacation. Set a financial goal and work together to meet that goal in the next six to twelve months.

Regardless of what you decide for your family, use the motto that got me (Josh) through my doctorate: "Today I will do what others won't, so tomorrow I can accomplish what others can't."[9]

What one activity will you commit to that will help cultivate patience in your life?

What one activity would your kids love that will require patience in both you and them?

Application

MORNING PRAYER

Father, patience requires contentment. I pray my kids won't become conceited, provoking one another, or envious. Help them "live by [and] keep in step with the Spirit" (Gal. 5:25-26).

DINNERTIME STORY

Tell your kids about a moment you felt proud of them for being patient. What specifically did they do and what was the outcome? Help them to see foresight and hindsight. What could have been the outcome had they not been patient in that moment? What good things happened because they were patient?

BEDTIME QUESTION

What is something you want me to know about being a kid your age?

ACTIVITY

My "Patience" Teacher: Even talking about ways of being patient gives our kids ideas for how to wait. Use drive time to ask them to teach you about ways they wait patiently. For instance, you may say, "Son, last night I noticed you decided to draw a picture while you waited for your sister to finish her chores. That's a great way to wait patiently. Can you tell me what you were drawing? I'd like to learn to be patient like that too."

Then, inquire about other ways your kids wait for things to happen. Let them become the teacher. Do they play games like "I Spy?" If so, ask them to teach you the game in the car. Do they make up songs while they wait? Make up songs on your drive. If your kids are too young to come up with their own ways of waiting, you become the teacher.

Day 5
Living with Eternity in Mind

Living in the here-and-now can be very difficult. Too often we find ourselves wishing we were further along with our careers, personal finances, relationships, or even our relationship with God.

I think that much of our discontentment comes from the fact that God placed eternity in our hearts (Eccl. 3:11), yet we live in the confines of time and space. And since we have a hard time making sense of eternity in our mundane, daily routines, pains, heartaches, and everyday inconveniences, we turn to other things to find significance and give us an identity.

For some of us, our identities become our future dreams. Not settled in the *now*, we daydream about and strive for the *not yet*. In the meantime, we miss what God has for us today—and today is all we're promised.

Since my dad died in November 2016, my (Josh) perspective has changed, and my patience in the day-to-day is growing. In Revelation 21:5, Jesus said,

> *Look, I am making everything new.*
> **REVELATION 21:5**

I know the struggle of making sure my kids do not disrespect or disobey me. We want our kids to listen. But when we live discontented lives, our fuses become quite short in the day-to-day. Instead of having patience to recognize that our kids—just like us—are still learning and developing, we act as if they too are a reason for our discontentment. Then, even the simplest provocation leads to yelling or words we later regret.

My dad was a man who made time for me. He was a man who never missed the moments. Did he have his flaws? Sure he did. But the one thing he showed me was that simply me being me was why he loved me. I can't wait to spend time with him when Jesus makes all things new.

As you help your kids learn patience, focus on the eternity placed in your heart. Be content that you don't have to do anything to earn your heavenly Father's love. When we lead our families with eternity in mind, the day-to-day becomes much more about who we are in Him, and less about who we're not to the world. That's a perspective our kids long for.

As you consider Revelation 21:5, what are some things you anticipate the Lord "making everything new"?

What do you most struggle with as it relates to living for eternity?

Write down three specific ways you can begin cultivating patience in your home and with your kids (e.g. more board games instead of screens, helping them learn things like playing piano or even tying a shoe, not waiting until the last minute and rushing everyone out the door, etc.).

1.

2.

3.

 Application

MORNING PRAYER

Lord Jesus, teach my children that "patience is better than power" (Prov. 16:32).

DINNERTIME STORY

Tell a story about when you had to be patient and wait on the Lord for an outcome. What did it feel like while you were waiting? What did "waiting patiently" look like for you? What was the outcome? Did God come through as you expected or differently? What did you learn about God during this time?

BEDTIME QUESTION

What's the most difficult part of being patient or waiting?

ACTIVITY

The Dream You Imagine: Kids lack peace for all sorts of reasons: the dark, monsters under their beds, the shadow on the wall, the bully at school, thunderstorms, being alone, going to school, not making the team, or being rejected by friends. Too often, our kids walk around with these fears, unable to verbalize them.

Tell your kids to use their imaginations to overcome a scenario of fear. Instead of being scared of the monster in the closet or the bully at school, help them devise a scheme where a superhero comes to the rescue. It could be a trusted friend or grown-up, or even themselves. Everybody take turns helping each other come up with a scenario to conquer their fears and then bring Jesus, through the Holy Spirit, into the situation.

Just allow your kids to talk about and imagine their scenarios for how it could be resolved. This alone reduces anxiety, fosters creativity, and brings peace to their minds. When we face our fears together, even the fear of being alone diminishes.

MORNING PRAYER

Today, Lord, help me as a parent to be patient with my children and have compassion toward their developing hearts and minds.

DINNERTIME STORY

Tell your kids about the coolest thing that happened to you today or this week.

BEDTIME QUESTION

How can I be more patient with you? Or, for younger children, ask: *What scares you or makes you sad?*

ACTIVITY

The Quiet Game: As you're driving, play the quiet game. Everyone stays quiet for as long as possible. The first person to make a noise or talks loses. You can either keep the game going by playing for points, or play together and try to beat a time as a family for staying quiet. Winners get a surprise for their patience.

Understanding My Child

From an early age, our children learn through story. A good children's Bible illustrates many of these stories. Reading biblical stories aloud together as a family is helpful for some kids. However, some children, especially during preschool ages, may grow bored. In this case, one of the best ways to teach our little ones these stories is to tell them ourselves.

Begin by reading a particular story from the Bible. Write down the key lesson from the story. Next, write down how you could age-appropriately communicate the key lesson to your children from facts of the story. Then, with your child, read the passage as you act it out. Use voice inflection to distinguish between characters. Move your hands. Use props from around the house. Bring your children into the story as characters.

If you're studying with a group, take some time to discuss a few of the concepts from last week's personal and family study. We'll provide some discussion points and questions each week on these pages to help guide your conversation.

1. Living with a Grateful Heart

Someone read Philippians 4:6-7 aloud.

What precedes the "peace that surpasses all understanding"?

How do the definitions of peace **affect your perspective on parenting?**

When do you feel most at peace?

2. Living with a Whole Heart

Discuss the story of Fernando. How does the phrase "one heart" speak to you about what it means to have peace with someone? With God?

How does Jesus help us have peace with God? How does He make our hearts whole?

How does Romans 5:1 confirm Jesus' title as the Prince of peace?

Talk about your own spiritual journey growing in peace. When did you feel peace even in a difficult time?

What has God been showing you about living at peace as an adult?

3. Living with a Present Mind

Someone read Ephesians 6:4 from The Message aloud (p. 60).

How have you helped unite your child's inner turmoil and bring peace to his or her heart and mind in anxious situations?

In what ways have you provoked anger in your child previously?

Who was a coach, teacher, pastor, or boss you had who seemed to live in peace? How did he or she teach this lesson to you?

4. Living with a Patient Attitude

What hard thing did you do at an early age that helped you develop patience?

How can you be more patient with your kids?

How did your parents (your kids' grandparents) show patience to you while you were growing up? Is there a moment you remember specifically when they showed patience to one another or to someone else in the family?

5. Living with Eternity in Mind

Someone read Colossians 3:1-4 aloud.

What's this passage telling you to focus your mind on? What is it telling you not to focus your mind on?

When you look at the conversation in your home, does your ongoing conversation reflect a Colossians 3:1-2 mind-set?

How do you see the conversation in your home needing to change to have your kids grow with an eternal mind-set?

How does an eternal mind-set compete with the instant gratification and comparison culture we find ourselves in today?

JUST AS

you want

OTHERS TO DO

for you,

DO THE SAME

for them.

LUKE 6:31

SESSION 4: KINDNESS + GOODNESS

Do you tend to overprioritize your kids' misbehavior? In other words, if you're anything like us, your tendency is to quickly come down hard on your child's misbehavior without giving thought to the motivation or reason behind the behavior.

For example, have you ever tried to get your child to behave when he or she was overtired? You try to teach a lesson in the moment only to witness a complete meltdown and repeated misbehavior. Instead of raising the white flag and chalking it up to tiredness, we feel we have to get our point across so our kids will learn to be "good." Unfortunately, these moments always seem to lead to yelling and a not-so-fun bedtime. You've been there too?

One of the most important lessons we're learning as parents is to focus on the motivation behind our kids doing good, not just getting them to behave for "goodness' sake." This is a distinct example of why the fruit of the Spirit is more than just character traits or behavior modification.

We can try to make our kids do good, but until they learn that rules are made out of love for them, they will not obey. You may have heard it said that rules without relationship lead to rebellion, but rules with relationship lead to respect.

When cultivating a relationship with our kids, we often ask ourselves, *Am I the adult I want my kids to grow up to be?* If we tell our kids to "be good" or to "kill them with kindness," are we doing the same to those with whom our children watch us interact? Or better yet, do we show our kids kindness when they are unkind toward us? This can be incredibly difficult to do, especially considering how many times a day our kids can tax our patience.

Remember, we *cultivate* goodness and kindness in our kids, and this takes time. In this session, we'll learn:

1. What kindness is
2. How to cultivate kindness in our kids
3. What goodness is
4. How to cultivate goodness in our kids
5. Why the Sabbath matters for fruit to grow

Day 1
What Is Kindness?

When you were growing up, do you remember being picked on at school or by a sibling? Somebody who really knew how to push your buttons? Perhaps your mom would say, "Kill them with kindness."

At first glance, the motive behind this phrase sounds quite harsh. But a further look into how we treat those who test our patience may actually prove the phrase quite accurate.

Read Romans 12:19-20.

> *Friends, do not avenge yourselves; instead, leave room for*
> *God's wrath, because it is written, Vengeance belongs to me;*
> *I will repay, says the Lord. But If your enemy is hungry, feed him.*
> *If he is thirsty, give him something to drink. For in so doing*
> *you will be heaping fiery coals on his head.*
> **ROMANS 12:19-20**

This verse follows several verses that teach us how to live as Christians in the world: "cling to what is good" (v. 9), "love one another deeply" (v. 10), "be fervent in the Spirit; serve the Lord" (v. 11), "rejoice in hope" (v. 12), "be patient," pray, "share with the saints" (v. 13), be hospitable, and "live in harmony with one another" (v. 16). Then at the end, Paul implored us to "live at peace with everyone" (v. 18), not trying to get vengeance ourselves. Instead, we should be kind to our enemies by providing for their needs. In so doing, we will be "heaping fiery coals on his head" (v. 20).

Paul borrowed that phrase from the Book of Proverbs (25:21-22), which gives advice for how to live in wisdom. While we should not wish fiery coals on our enemies' heads, we should understand that it's wise to treat them with kindness because we have also been treated with undue kindness. Earlier in Romans, Paul wrote:

> *Or do you despise the riches of his kindness, restraint,*
> *and patience, not recognizing that God's kindness*
> *is intended to lead you to repentance?*
> **ROMANS 2:4**

God's kindness to us leads us to repentance. As a reflection of Him, when we treat others kindly, we may serve as catalysts for their repentance as well.

The Greek root for *kindness* in Galatians 5:22 means uprightness, or benevolence, and describes "the ability to act for the welfare of those taxing our patience."[1]

What about this definition stands out the most to you?

How can you apply this definition in your relationships with your kids?

Do you, as an adult, think it's difficult being kind? Why or why not?

Kindness comes quite unnatural to humans. When we have been hurt, we tend to react in hurt. But kindness is the opposite. It inspires us to bless others. For example, kindness is when your child, though treated badly by a friend or sibling, still shares gummy bears with them at snack time. Kindness is when you as a parent, though your child speaks disrespectfully at you, choose not to speak harshly back.[2]

As you get started in leading your kids in kindness, help them memorize Proverbs 16:24— "Pleasant words are a honeycomb: sweet to the taste and health to the body." We had our kids memorize it and learn about what the bee makes—honey. Now, when they say unkind words to one another, we ask about the bee and the sweet honey it makes.

Kind words and honey. A sweet taste for the soul. Health for the body.

So often we focus more on what our kids are doing wrong rather than what they're doing right. What kind words do your kids use? How can you better encourage them in their words?

 Application

MORNING PRAYER

Father, may my kids be commended for their kindness.

DINNERTIME STORY

Tell your kids about a moment you felt proud of them for being kind toward someone, especially if that person was taxing your child's patience. What specifically did your child do to be kind? Point out what you noticed about that moment and how you saw kindness play out in them.

BEDTIME QUESTION

Can you tell me about a time when someone was unkind to you? How did it make you feel?

ACTIVITY

Pay It Forward: This is a game where you do a random act of kindness. This is one you can do for drive time as well. Let everyone—either upon waking up, eating breakfast, or in the car on the drive to school—take turns talking about what act they will do.

For instance, if you're at the grocery store, offer to carry someone's groceries. If you're at the drive-through window, pay for the car behind you. You could buy coupons for a car wash and randomly give them away to someone you see. Perhaps you open the door for your mom or dad before they get into the car. Better yet, maybe you get into your seat quickly and neatly without a fuss to be kind to your parents. Here are a few other options:

- Hold the door
- Carry groceries
- Give away coupons
- Buy someone's meal
- Smile at and say hi to the people you meet
- Say please and thank you
- Speak respectfully to adults
- Help your teacher at school
- Ask someone if they need help

Day 2
How to Cultivate Kindness in Our Kids

Here are a few ways to cultivate kindness in our kids:

- Internalizing Scripture
- Speaking kindness
- Praying for those who tax our kids' patience
- Being a kind and loyal friend
- Showing hospitality

Read Luke 6:27-36. List three takeaways from this passage about being kind to others.

1.

2.

3.

One of the conditions we implemented for our children to get out of time-out is to have them tell us, using a Bible verse, the lesson they learned. A few verses they readily choose include Proverbs 16:24; Luke 6:31; and Philippians 2:3.

Write down three verses you would like your children to internalize that relate to how they treat others. We use the word *internalize* because this isn't just about memorization—it's about living the verse out in their everyday lives.

1.

2.

3.

When it comes to cultivating fruit in our home, our own branches can all too often grow quite a few thorns on them.

When our kids tax our patience, we tend to take it out on our spouse. Perhaps we use unkind words or tone of voice.

To instill kindness in our kids requires that we watch our own tongues. When we get to the end of our patience rope, so often we treat those we love the most as our enemies instead of loved ones. But in light of Luke 6:27-36, there's never an excuse to speak unkind words. Instead, take a deep breath and act for the good of *their* welfare.

Who do you have the most difficult time being kind to? (You don't have to list their names here, but keep them in mind.) Is there a particular situation, time of day, or circumstance when you tend to become more unkind?

What about for your children? Do you see patterns in them when they are unkind more than at other times? What's happening in their lives at this moment (e.g. overtired from a long day, hungry, been around people too much, no nap, immediately following school, etc.)?

How can you see these patterns and help them not become so overwhelmed or self-focused?

If you're raising boys, the tendency may be to see kindness as too soft. Yet our culture has confused the definition of what it means to be a man. Think about what it means to be a man based on God's unfathomable kindness to unbelievers, a kindness to those who didn't love Him, a kindness that expects nothing in return (Rom. 2:4; Eph. 2:7). Picture Jesus on the cross, kindly praying for the soldiers murdering Him (Luke 23:34).

For many men, our initial reaction is that if we're kind and don't stand up for ourselves, others will walk all over us. But isn't that the upside-down kingdom of God?

> *The last will be first, and the first last.*
> **MATTHEW 20:16**

> *Love your enemies and pray for those who persecute you.*
> **MATTHEW 5:44**

Think about those who tax our patience. A coworker. Our boss. The person who cut us off on the highway. Our spouse. Our kids. Let's model what Jesus did and pray for them.

With your kids, especially when someone is taxing their patience, have them ask God to reveal a new way of looking at the situation. This often changes how we respond to and view that individual and their situation.

Read Matthew 8:1-4. What do you notice about Jesus in this situation?

How have you used the kindness of touch to bless another? How can you model this for your kids?

Read 1 Samuel 20, especially paying attention to verses 14-17.

We live in a culture of comfort. However, loving others costs us something. For example, taking care of a sick friend means we have to give up our time. David and Jonathan had a deep friendship.

Do you have friendships based on such loyalty and kindness?

How can you help your kids develop such friendships? Who are the people your kids are surrounded by? Do they produce good fruit?

 Application

MORNING PRAYER

Lord God, help my children to do to others as they would have others do to them (Luke 6:31).

DINNERTIME STORY

Talk about how you as a family will commit one act of kindness a day for the next week. Work as a family team. Will you use a point system? How many points will your family try to get by the end of the month? Use dinnertime to talk about how you will achieve a daily act of kindness each day as a family. Consider journaling your journey and praying for those taxing your patience.

BEDTIME QUESTION

Who are kids in school, at church, on your teams, or in your neighborhood who are kind to you?

ACTIVITY

Daily Act of Kindness: Each morning throughout this week, spend time thinking about one act of kindness you could show another that particular day. Ask God to open your eyes for those who need kindness. Then, on your drive home from school or during dinnertime, tell the story of your act of kindness for the day.

To make it a game, create a weekly chart for your family. Keep a tally of who is most consistent, and who scores the most creative and helpful acts of kindness each day. Who went above and beyond for someone taxing his or her patience? To work as a family team, set a goal of thirty acts of kindness as a family and work hard to reach your goal. You can also write down the names of the people whom you bless and pray for them each night.

Day 3
What Is Goodness?

Remember, the fruit of the Spirit are interconnected. None of us can develop the fruit of the Spirit without the Spirit.

It takes time. It takes a lot of time to watch trees grow, just as it takes time to watch goodness grow in your kids. You can measure their growth over time, but you can't sit and watch them grow. As much as we'd love to see our kids become embodiments of goodness, true goodness birthed from the Spirit of God happens in time.

> **Read Mark 10:17-22. What about Jesus' response to the man surprises you?**

Jesus' reply to the rich young ruler is fascinating: "'Why do you call me good?' Jesus asked him. 'No one is good except God alone'" (Mark 10:18). The young ruler had followed all of God's commandments, yet it wasn't enough. Jesus told him, "Go, sell all you have and give to the poor, and you will have treasure in heaven. Then come, follow me." (Mark 10:21).

In his question, the rich young ruler asked how to do good, using a Greek word referring to moral behavior. However, the *goodness* described as a fruit of the Spirit means much more. The fruit of goodness is excellence of character. It combines our attempts to *do good* with God's character of *being good*.[3]

> **Read 2 Peter 1:3. How do we obtain what is necessary for life and godliness?**

Finish reading 2 Peter 1:3-11. What are we told to "supplement" our faith with (v. 5)?

Based on Peter's words, how do we maintain this goodness over time?

Teaching our children to just "do good" can look very much like legalism—especially when we only reward them for good behavior. The rich young ruler was trying to do good to earn his way into heaven, yet he was lacking the most important thing—an underlying love for the Rule Maker. This love is what "compels us" to follow the rules in the first place (2 Cor. 5:14).

We see here how, once again, the fruit of the Spirit are interconnected. It begins with love. Without love, you can do good, but the goodness isn't complete. Like the rich young ruler, this goodness is based on what one can get out of it. But Jesus told the rich young ruler that he couldn't have it his way and still gain eternal life without an underlying love for Him.

As much as we'd like to think that our kids obey us because they love us, this ultimately doesn't come until later in childhood. The same can be said for our faith. We grow obedient over time as we fall more in love with the Rule Maker Himself.

Goodness doesn't come by our strength alone—only God's. As you seek goodness, pray that God gives you the strength to choose goodness—to the poor, the hurting, and especially your spouse and kids. Not merely because it's what you're supposed to do, but because God loves you enough that He already shows the same goodness toward you.

 Application

MORNING PRAYER

Dear God, help my children to supplement their faith with goodness (2 Pet. 1:5).

DINNERTIME STORY

Read your children the story of the good Samaritan (Luke 10:25-37). Tell your children a modern-day good Samaritan story, where either you were the good Samaritan or were on the receiving end of a good Samaritan.

BEDTIME QUESTION

How does it make you feel when someone (Mom, Dad, your teacher, pastor, etc.) tells you that you did a good job?

ACTIVITY

I Failed. I Learned! The point of this game is to reward creativity and celebrate failure. Many times, we feel ashamed when we think we failed at something, especially if it was a moment when we could have shown goodness to another person. But what if we celebrated these moments as opportunities to learn and grow?

Everyone take a turn either describing a moment they saw someone else not do good to someone or describe a moment they could have done good but didn't (Prov. 3:27). For example, "Yesterday I saw an elderly woman carrying groceries to her car in the pouring rain. Instead of going to help her I just hurried past because I was running late. I still feel badly about it."

After that, everyone comes up with lessons we can learn about that moment. Remember, failing isn't the problem. It's when we fail to learn from our failures that will make life most difficult. Use this game to teach your kids to pay attention to the opportunities of doing good to and loving others.

Day 4
How to Cultivate Goodness in Our Kids

The clearest example of kindness and goodness in Scripture is the parable of the good Samaritan, who not only stopped to help the half-dead Jewish man, but also paid for his care.

Read Luke 10:25-37.

Write down your greatest takeaway from this parable.

The good Samaritan did not help in order to earn his way to heaven. The goodness he showed sprung from the kindness within his heart—concern for the Jewish man's well-being, despite his own personal expense.

Name someone who goes above and beyond for others, like the good Samaritan.

Write down a modern-day good Samaritan story, where either you were the good Samaritan or were on the receiving end of a good Samaritan.

How have you recently lived out goodness? What decision did you make? What were the alternative decisions that you could have made?

Similar to the "I Failed. I Learned!" game in the Day 3 application, talk about a time when you wish you would have or could have done good for somebody. What lessons did you learn from that moment? How will you make sure you recognize these moments again in the future so as to act on them?

Instilling kindness and goodness in our children begins by our modeling loving behavior through our family values. Dr. John Gottman, one of the world's renowned marital researchers, describes it as creating "shared meaning" together in marriage.[4] In other words, establishing values you live and lead by in your marriage.

Write down two or three clear values your family lives by. If you don't have values written down, take some time to talk to your spouse about the family values you believe you already live by based on the decisions you currently make as a family.

What two or three core values do you want your family to live by?

Start with your marriage. With or without your kids, find another couple, family, or person whose well-being you and your spouse are concerned about. Center a date night or family outing when you can serve them together. How will you serve them? Is cooking a family strength? Hospitality? Acts of service, like raking their lawn? Find the gifts and passions God has given your family and find how you can serve them. This is how we begin to create shared meaning—and purpose—in our families.

 Application

MORNING PRAYER

Heavenly Father, multiply the fruit and work of my children's hands. Give me insight and understanding to raise my children in such a way that they hear those most coveted words, "Well done, good and faithful servant!" (Matt. 25:21).

DINNERTIME STORY

Imagine someone walked in and gave your family (not just you) $20,000. You were only allowed to spend it on doing good for others. What good could you do with that money?

BEDTIME QUESTION

What's something you recently did that was good? Not because you followed the rules but because you knew it was the right thing to do?

ACTIVITY

Ripple Effects: Ask your kids, *Do our actions over time cause ripple effects on others?* Of course they do.

Fill the sink with water. Find different-weighted objects to drop into the water. For instance, find something heavy, like a spoon or even a weighted piece of dough. How many ripples did it make? Go down in weighted objects, pointing out the decreasing number of ripples. Try a Hershey's Kiss®. Then, drop in a bean. Go as small as a chocolate chip or sprinkle. Use this illustration to show that no matter what we drop in, it makes a ripple.

Use examples of how happy they are when someone gives them a smile (a chocolate chip), a compliment (a bean), a Christmas present (a Hershey Kiss), or cleans their bedroom (a spoon). Even though a chocolate chip makes fewer ripples, more smiles over time add up to the number of ripples of a spoon. Even the smallest of actions, done often over time, have ripple effects on the lives of so many.

Day 5

Why the Sabbath Matters for Fruit to Grow

Did you know that plants, trees, and other vegetation need rest to grow healthy? Let's use a fruit tree for example. During the day, the fruit tree uses sunlight for photosynthesis. If the tree never gets rest from the sunlight, the growth process stops because the water the tree receives begins being used to cool the plant tissue from all of the heat energy rather than being used for the growth process. Trees need darkness to regenerate phytochrome and keep growing.

As humans, we, too, need to pay attention when we need rest.

Jesus declared,

> *The Sabbath was made for man and not man for the Sabbath.*
> **MARK 2:27**

What do you think it means that the Sabbath was made for humans?

If the Sabbath was made for us, why do we so often neglect it?

How is your Sabbath life? What about for your family? How well, on a scale of 1 to 10, 10 being every single week, do you practice the Sabbath? Describe what your Sabbath consists of (worship, hobbies besides work, rest, time with family, etc.).

1   2   3   4   5   6   7   8   9   10

Read Genesis 1–2:3, paying particular attention to and emphasizing every time the word good *is used.*

Did God need to rest? Was He tired from creating the world?

God didn't need to rest, but instead, He created the Sabbath so that we could rest and take delight in the good we are doing. Notice the pattern that develops in how God took delight in all of the good He created. In a culture that rarely slows down long enough to celebrate, use the activity on the next page as a way to instill a culture of celebration in your home.

How often do you and your spouse take time to rest and celebrate all that God is doing in your marriage?

How do you celebrate all of the good God is doing in the work each of you puts your hands to?

As humans, our bodies need rest. Only in that rest can we take the time to remember the good that God is doing in our lives. To continuously keep working and fail to celebrate makes us no different than a machine. Machines never stop. Machines never celebrate.

As a human being (not human doing) establish the created pattern of the Sabbath in your home. Celebrate the good God is doing in and through your family. Establish it for your kids early on, and it will be a practice they value and keep holy throughout their lifetimes (Ex. 20:8).

Application

MORNING PRAYER

God, make my children worthy of their calling, and by Your power, fulfill their every desire to do good, so that the name of the our Lord Jesus will be glorified by them.

DINNERTIME STORY

Tell your kids a story about a friend or mentor who stood up for you at school, church, or with others. Who were the kind kids? Who did right (good) by you? Do you still know them today?

BEDTIME QUESTION

Do you think it's hard being good? Why or why not?

ACTIVITY

Celebrate the Good! Read Genesis 1–2:3, the story of creation to your kids. Emphasize every statement where God says the word *good*. Explain to your kids that God didn't need to rest, but He created the Sabbath so that we could rest and take delight in the good that we are doing. In a culture that rarely slows down long enough to celebrate, use this activity as a way to instill a culture of celebration in your home.

Everybody take a turn talking about something good they accomplished this past week— it could be a project at school that went well, sharing lunch with a friend, or sharing toys with a sibling.

Everybody finish the sentence, "I want to celebrate that I was able to _____ this week." Everybody go around and honor the person. Celebrate the good they did. Ask questions. Talk about the positive ramifications of what they did, and how it might have made someone else feel or influenced them to make a better decision.

Once everyone has had a turn to celebrate the good he or she has done, put someone on the hot seat, and have everyone take turns celebrating the good that person has done through the eyes of others that week. For example, "Sarah, I want to celebrate how you took the time to notice my new haircut. It really meant a lot that you noticed and went out of your way to tell me how nice I look."

 Bonus Application

MORNING PRAYER

God, I praise You today because my kids are remarkably and wondrously made. Their bones are not hidden from You. You created their "inward parts." You knit them together in the womb. Their days were already "written in your book and planned before a single one of them began." Help me to trust You with them, Lord (Ps. 139:13-16).

DINNERTIME STORY

Age-appropriately, share with your kids what God is teaching you right now in your life.

BEDTIME QUESTION

Is there someone at your school who isn't very popular? What can you do tomorrow to brighten his or her day?

ACTIVITY

Let Your Light Shine: Gather as many flashlights, lanterns, or lights that have bulbs as you can find in your house. Put them on the table. If you have lights with varying filters and colors, all the better. Turn the lights on.

Discuss with your kids the differences with each one (colors, sizes, designs, etc.). Tell them to walk around and look at floor and table lamps too. Talk about or write down the differences.

Which flashlight is their favorite? Is there a lamp they find ugly or wouldn't use? Direct your kids to pick the light they find the ugliest and have them sit with it in the living room. Read 1 Samuel 16:7 together. Ask what all of the lights have in common—a light bulb. Explain that no matter how popular, good looking, talented, or rich people are on the outside, God looks at the light they shine—through their hearts. Though David was the youngest of his brothers and not the one most would have expected to be king, God looked at his heart, not his "outward appearance" (2 Cor. 5:12).

Understanding My Child

As parents, one of the best ways to cultivate a love for the Bible in our kids is to show them how we read, pray through, and learn from it. Don't be shy about sharing with your child what God is teaching you. Our children aren't born knowing that our basis for right and wrong is the Bible. We have to show them.

Use dinnertime or bedtime to help your children see how a decision you recently made was based on a particular truth from the Bible. When our children make the connection between our actions and the truth of the Bible, they begin to see the fruit of the Spirit lived out before them in the hearts of others.

Write down a few recent decisions you made that tie to a truth in the Bible or a fruit you lived out. For example, you chose not to gossip about someone (Eph. 4:29), you took an extra shift at work because your family needed the money (Prov. 6:6), you complimented your spouse (Prov. 16:24), or you took dinner to a family in need (Gal. 5:13). Review highlights of your day over dinner or at bedtime to communicate these decisions and their biblical connections to your children.

_____

_____

_____

_____

_____

_____

_____

_____

_____

_____

_____

If you're studying with a group, take some time to discuss a few of the concepts from last week's personal and family study. We'll provide some discussion points and questions each week on these pages to help guide your conversation.

1. What Is Kindness?

Someone read Galatians 5:22 aloud.

What about the definition of *kindness* stands out to you the most?

Do you, as an adult, think it's difficult being kind? Why or why not?

In what ways has God been kind to you? Think in terns of when you have taxed His patience.

In your own words, what's the difference between being nice and being kind?

2. How to Cultivate Kindness in Our Kids

Someone read Luke 6:27-36 aloud.

Talk about your takeaways from this passage about being kind to others.

Is there a particular situation, time of day, or circumstance when you tend to become unkind more than at others?

What about for your children? Do you see patterns in them when they are unkind more than at other times? What can you share with the group that has helped your children not to become overwhelmed during these times?

3. What Is Goodness?

Read Mark 10:17-22. What about Jesus' response to the man surprises you?

Read 2 Peter 1:3. How do we obtain what is necessary for life and godliness?

Finish reading 2 Peter 1:3-11. What are we told to "supplement" our faith with (v. 5)?

Based on Peter's words, how do we maintain this goodness over time?

4. How to Cultivate Goodness in Our Kids

Someone read Luke 10:25-37 aloud.

What's your biggest takeaway from this parable?

When was the last time you wish you would have or could have been a good Samaritan? What lessons did you learn from that moment? How will you make sure you recognize these moments again in the future so as to act on them?

Share with the group one or more of the family values you wrote down or brainstormed this week.

5. Why the Sabbath Matters for Fruit to Grow

Jesus declared in Mark 2:27, "The Sabbath was made for man and not man for the Sabbath."

What do you think it means that the Sabbath was made for humans?

If the Sabbath was made for us, why do we so often neglect it?

What's the ideal Sabbath for you and your family?

NOW FAITH IS THE

reality

OF WHAT IS HOPED FOR,

the proof of

WHAT IS

not seen.

HEBREWS 11:1

SESSION 5: FAITHFULNESS + GENTLENESS

When your child is passionate about one particular gift for Christmas or a birthday, do you do all you can to get it for him or her? Assuming it's within budget, there's not a loving parent in the world who wants to withhold good gifts from his or her child.

Look at what Jesus says about this, "Who among you, if his son asks him for bread, will give him a stone? Or if he asks for a fish, will give him a snake? If you then, who are evil, know how to give good gifts to your children, how much more will your Father in heaven give good things to those who ask him" (Matt. 7:9-11). Even more so than an earthly father, God remains faithful to those whose faith is in Him.

God's faithfulness to us is the reason we can walk in the Holy Spirit to begin with. Jesus says, "No one can come to me unless the Father who sent me draws him" (John 6:44). Walking in faithfulness begins by realizing that faith, in and of itself, is a gift from our faithful, loving Father in heaven. Consider some of the ways God is faithful to you: He will never "leave you or abandon you" (Deut. 31:6; Heb. 13:5); He gave up His only Son that you might be saved (John 3:16); He is your Good Shepherd who knows you intimately (Ps. 23:1; Isa. 40:11; John 10:14); He takes care of you (Matt. 6:25-34); "he is faithful and righteous to forgive us our sins" (1 John 1:9); He keeps His promises (Gen. 9:12-17).

Faithfulness may arguably be the fruit all others hinge on. The fruit of the Spirit is harvested in those who are saved. Every follower of Jesus is "saved by grace through faith" (Eph. 2:8), and "without faith it is impossible to please God" (Heb. 11:6). Seeing faith as a marvelous gift from God is the beginning of being children of God who are faithful and trustworthy in return. The more we experience and press into God's faithfulness toward us, the more we grow into children He can trust to obey Him.

Furthermore, Jesus, in spite of how He was treated, was without sin, gentle, meek, and lowly in heart (Matt. 11:29). Our ever-growing faith also gives us the strength to respond to others in gentleness. But what this requires of us once again is surrender.

Here's what we'll learn:
1. How to cultivate faithfulness in our kids
2. What gentleness is
3. How to cultivate gentleness in our kids
4. Being teachable
5. Being faithful to what matters most

Day 1

How to Cultivate Faithfulness in Our Kids

Our son had a difficult journey in preschool. For whatever reason, we learned that he was terrified of making a mistake. It would paralyze him from engaging the material or learning.

Since he was in preschool we decided to pull him out and put him into a different preschool that was less structured for the rest of that year. As we prayed about his kindergarten year (where he would go all day, every day) we knew he needed a gentle teacher who would understand his fear and help him understand that it's OK to make mistakes.

Should we homeschool? Send him to public school? Find a private school? We were deep in prayer for our boy. Part way through the following year God placed our neighbor—who was a substitute teacher looking to engage a full-time position again after raising her kids, and who happened to be one of the safest people in our son's life—into a kindergarten class in our local school after another teacher quit her position. You can imagine the rest of the story. Our son had our neighbor for his kindergarten teacher.

As a parent, you feel everything your kids feel. When they hurt, you hurt. And in the trials, we often try to do all we can to gain some level of control, forgetting that God promised He would never leave us or forsake us.

We have to do our part in turning our eyes toward heaven.

Therefore we do not give up. Even though our outer person is being destroyed, our inner person is being renewed day by day. For our momentary light affliction is producing for us an absolutely incomparable eternal weight of glory. So we do not focus on what is seen, but on what is unseen. For what is seen is temporary, but what is unseen is eternal.
2 CORINTHIANS 4:16-18

What's your tendency in a "momentary light affliction" (which never feels light and momentary at the time!) with your kids? Do you try to handle the situation on your own? Do you focus on the seen? Or do you turn to the unseen first, giving it to God in prayer and staying steadfast in it, knowing He is faithful and loves your kids more than you do?

What's the most difficult part of believing that God will remain faithful to you and your family?

God wants to use every part of your child's story for His glory.

What part of your child's story have you not considered as a blessing or seen God's faithfulness in?

How can you begin to champion that part of your child's story for God's glory?

Even when our children sin and are unfaithful, our faithfulness to our kids should leave us shamelessly running, arms wide open to receive our child back into our loving arms (see Luke 15:11-32).

In the moments when your kids sin, don't turn to your fears of how your kids will turn out. Turn to the unseen, in prayer for your kids, by faith, confidently believing that God will carry out the good work He has started in your kids (Phil. 1:6).

How has God been faithful to you and your family?

Tell a story about a moment when you felt proud of your kids for being faithful to God, especially when others may have been doing the wrong thing. What specifically did they do to walk in faithfulness?

If you're married, share a story about how God has been faithful in your marriage.

How can you help your spouse grow closer to God? What does your spouse say he or she needs to increase in faithfulness?

Talk about your own spiritual journey growing in faithfulness. What has God been showing you about walking in faith as an adult?

Read John 14:23.

Jesus answered, "If anyone loves me, he will keep my word. My Father will love him, and we will come to him and make our home with him."
JOHN 14:23

Shortly after this Jesus promised us the Holy Spirit, who will come and teach us these things.

But the Counselor, the Holy Spirit, whom the Father will send in my name, will teach you all things and remind you of everything I have told you.
JOHN 14:26

I (Josh) am in a season where I'm surrendering my fears to God. When I allow fears to creep into my life, I tend to take control and fail to trust that God can handle it. To increase my faith requires that I regularly confess my unbelief.

Do an inventory of the places where you fail to trust God. Write them down.

How can you walk in concert with the Holy Spirit to teach and remind you of the things Jesus said about who He is?

Ask the Holy Spirit to increase your faithfulness.

Helping our children walk in faithfulness begins by praying for them to receive the gift of faith from God. For that faith to increase, we want to be parents who can recognize in our children the places they lack trust and model for them what a life of faithfulness to God looks like.

 # Application

MORNING PRAYER

Holy Spirit, increase my faithfulness and give my kids a keen ear and watchful eye to the moments I get it right.

DINNERTIME STORY

Tell your children a story about the day they were born or their "gotcha day." As you tell the story leading up to their birth or their coming into your family, highlight the God moments, or markers of His faithfulness, that you look back on with gratitude. Were they prayed for before you even knew about them? Who played a role in their coming into your family (doctors, nurses, case workers, social workers, temporary caretakers, birth mothers, etc.)? Did someone pray for you as you became parents of this child? Who came to see you in the hospital or to welcome you home?

BEDTIME QUESTION

Describe what it means to be faithful to God. How can we be faithful to Him?

ACTIVITY

Establishing Values: How we prioritize our loyalties can be the difference between being a frantic family or a faithful family devoted to established priorities. As a family, come up with three to five values that you want to live by. You may already be living by these values but just want to be accountable to them even more. When we write out our values, it puts on paper a direction.

Ask as a family, *What makes us unique?* In other words, *What is God calling our family to be (and do) for His glory?*

Begin to write down words that describe your family and make you unique. Tell your kids to do the same. Use drive time to have these discussions. What made you choose these values? How do your kids see these values in your family? We recommend Patrick Lencioni's book on this topic called *The 3 Big Questions for a Frantic Family*.

Once you have established your values, begin putting action steps under each value. For instance, if faith is a value of your family, you might write that you will attend church every Sunday, join a small group, or read the Bible as a family for twenty minutes a day as action steps.

Day 2
What Is Gentleness?

We recently got a puppy. His name is Copper. Knowing he needed to be trained, we took Copper to our friend, Russell, who trains dogs as a hobby. Russell has a big yellow Labrador Retriever named Maggie whom he used to help train Copper. What we learned is that training our puppy with another well-trained dog was important. As Russell told us, "My dog won't put up with puppy behavior, but he's also gentle enough not to hurt Copper, even though he could."

That's a beautiful picture of gentleness. Gentleness is not weakness. In fact, the people who need to pay attention to being gentle are those with the most strength, like Maggie.

The Greek word for gentleness in Galatians 5:23 is *prautés*, and also means "meekness" or "gentle strength."[1] Helping our kids understand that gentleness is not a sign of being weak, but actually being strong, is an important place to begin when teaching them what it means to be gentle.

Think about when your child is angry. Does an angry response in return by us—a parent in power—have a soothing effect on our child's anger? If it's anything like our kids' anger, things go downhill from there. Solomon wrote,

> *A gentle answer turns away anger, but a harsh word stirs up wrath.*
> **PROVERBS 15:1**

Do you see the power in being gentle? We can teach our kids how to calm another person down by being gentle. But it takes great strength and self-control (another fruit of the Spirit) to speak a gentle word, especially if the other person isn't being so kind toward us.

Read James 1:19-20. What's required of us to be gentle?

What's the opposite response of gentleness?

In your own life, do you consider yourself generally gentle in response to others or angry when you feel wronged or not understood?

That leads to the question, where do we get the strength to give a gentle response?

First, it comes from surrendering our flesh to the Holy Spirit (Gal. 5:24-25). Physically taking a step back, saying a prayer, taking deep breaths, and waiting thirty seconds to respond can be the difference between an angry reaction and gentle response.

The strength it takes to be gentle also comes in humility. As Puritan Jonathan Edwards described it, we have to be willing to think of ourselves less (humility) so that we can see into the world of other people and act on their behalf (gentleness).[2]

We may or may not immediately think of God as gentle, but He is the ultimate example of strength and gentleness. The Bible often highlights both aspects of this when referring to God as our Shepherd.

Read Psalm 23; Isaiah 40:11; and John 10:11.

When have you experienced God as a gentle Shepherd? How has God gently cared for you in your walk with Him?

Have you seen gentleness as a strength or a weakness? Why?

Teach your kids, whenever they're quick to speak, slow to listen, and quick to anger, to take a step back, and in humility, think about how they can bring calm to the situation by "a gentle answer" (Prov. 15:1).

 # Application

MORNING PRAYER

Heavenly Father, thank You for never breaking Your promises to us. Help my children to remember they can trust You in all circumstances.

DINNERTIME STORY

Share with your children stories about how God has been faithful in your life and to your family. Make God's faithfulness real to your kids tonight.

BEDTIME QUESTION

When you disobey God, or Mom and Dad, how does it make you feel? (If appropriate, read 1 John 1:9 and pray for forgiveness together tonight). Remind your kids of God's faithfulness when we confess our sins to Him.

ACTIVITY

A Trip Down Memory Lane: This activity is designed as an opportunity to show your kids the beauty of faithfulness in human relationships. Begin by choosing a relationship that you cherish and has demonstrated faithfulness from the beginning. This may be your relationship and faithfulness to your kids or to your spouse; it may be the faithful, sustaining friendship of a childhood or college friend. You could choose your own parents or a mentor who has remained faithful to loving and supporting you through the years.

Once you choose the relationship you hold so dear, find pictures or videos through the years you have with that person. If you want to show how faithful you are as a parent, show your child pictures and videos from the day he or she was born, or your "gotcha day," leading up to today. Talk about the key moments of transition when you were so proud of them. If you're married and you choose to highlight the relationship with your spouse, take time to read your wedding vows to your kids. If you have a video of your wedding or videos of a mentor, childhood friend, or a grandparent, show your kids. Use this as an opportunity to show your kids the power of what it means to be faithful in our closest relationships.

Day 3
How to Cultivate Gentleness in Our Kids

As a wife and mom, it's hard for me (Christi) to sometimes let things go, especially if someone wronged my children or my husband. I find I forgive others more easily if they wrong me, but when they wrong the people I love, I seem to have a more difficult time forgiving and giving my anger to the Lord.

Leave it to Jesus to once again challenge who I am in Him. In the Beatitudes, Jesus declared,

> *Blessed are the humble, for they will inherit the earth.*
> **MATTHEW 5:5**

The Greek word for *humble* here means, "God's strength under His control." Or more practically written, "Demonstrating power without undue harshness."[3]

When we've been wronged, we have power. How do you exert your power in these situations? Give an example.

What's difficult about forgiving someone?

When we've been wronged or hurt in some way, we feel a sense of righteous indignation. We quickly want to defend our loved ones or ourselves and right the wrong at best, or seek revenge, at worst. Yet, Jesus' words challenge us to look beyond our own selfish desires—our right to be right in the situation or even our right to seek revenge.

Instead, when we submit to the Holy Spirit, our humility moves us from thinking of ourselves to thinking about the other person. In other words, we give the person who wronged us the benefit of the doubt.

Instead, when we submit to the Holy Spirit, our humility moves us from thinking of ourselves to thinking about the other person. In other words, we give the person who wronged us the benefit of the doubt.

Rather than jumping into an accusatory tone, you try to understand why your husband wasn't very kind to you or engaging on a double date with friends. Rather than yelling or sending your kids to bed early for their erratic and childish behavior, you take a moment to consider if they need food, more rest, focused attention, or are just being kids. And rather than being passive aggressive toward a friend who hurt you, you pursue the friendship and ask her how she's doing.

Giving others the benefit of the doubt doesn't mean we're ignoring others' sins or getting walked on like a doormat. That's weakness. Gentleness comes from strength.

Early church father Aquinas likened the word *humility* in the Beatitudes to his Christian virtue of *magnanimity*, or in the English, *magnanimous*, which means "generous in forgiving an insult or injury."[4] It doesn't mean we don't forgive; it means we're generous in doing so.

In humility, give others the benefit of the doubt and the reward—"inherit the earth"—will be unmatched (Matt. 5:5).

Read John 7:53–8:11.

How did Jesus respond to the woman's sin? Put yourself in this moment. Based on what you know about Jesus from Scripture, how do you imagine Jesus' tone of voice, nonverbal expressions, and demeanor toward the woman?

What do you take away from this situation that applies to how you talk to your kids about their sin?

Do you have trouble giving your kids the benefit of the doubt when they misbehave (not being gentle enough)? Or, on the flip side, do you tend to give your kids too much benefit of the doubt to the point of excusing sin (being overly gentle but not faithful to their character)?

On a video screen at our wedding reception, God gave me (Josh) a gift I'll never forget.

As we finished dinner, our attention was turned to footage of Christi, at three-years-old, this innocent little girl sitting in the bathtub with her mom by her side, splashing water, and singing as if there wasn't a care in the world:

"And so I thank the Lord,
 For giving me the things I need,
 The sun, the rain, and the appleseed,
 The Lord is good to me."[5]

Just two weeks later, on the last day of our honeymoon, we found ourselves in the middle of the biggest argument we have had to date. As I sat across from her at dinner defending my perspective, Christi's eyes welled up with tears. Without warning, my mind replayed that precious footage of my wife singing, and my defense diminished. My argument no longer mattered.

How did I become hard and insensitive to the one person I love the most? Rather than being quick to listen, slow to speak, and slow to become angry (Jas. 1:19), I was quick to defend myself, quick to cast blame, and slow to be *gentle*.

So how can families develop gentleness toward one another?

The famous preacher A. W. Tozer wrote that one of the five keys to a deeper spiritual life is "never defend yourself. We're all born with a desire to defend ourselves. And if you insist upon defending yourself, God will let you do it. But if you turn the defence of yourself over to God He will defend you."[6]

When we work to defend ourselves, we put up emotional guards that make us hard and self-centered. In turn, we cast blame in an attempt to protect just one person—*me*.

When I saw the innocence and purity of three-year-old Christi during our argument, I began to understand that that little girl still lives inside of her, and it's my responsibility to handle her heart with care. Because she had given me her heart, she was now more emotionally vulnerable to me than anyone else in the world.

How can you be gentler toward your spouse this week? Your kids? Be as specific as possible.

Gentleness doesn't depend on who is right but on lowering our defenses and protecting the hearts of those we love the most.

This month, go back and watch childhood videos or look at pictures of one another as a way to instill gentleness with the innocent little girl or boy who still lives inside your spouse.[7] You might also do this with videos and pictures of your older kids. Remember when they were small and needed you to be gentle? They still need that.

Application

MORNING PRAYER

Lord God, I pray my children will "walk by faith, not by sight" (2 Cor. 5:7). May they live to please You in all things.

DINNERTIME STORY

Ahead of dinner this evening, ask everyone to list the top five things they are thankful for because of God's faithfulness. Go around the table and present your lists to one another, talking about why you're grateful for each one and how God has been faithful to you. When you're finished, talk about ways you can grow in your own trust and faithfulness toward God.

BEDTIME QUESTION

When I take you on our next date, just the two of us, what is it that you want to do together?

ACTIVITY

Rewrite Psalm 136: Yes, you read that correctly. Take time to read Psalm 136 as a family. This psalm tells the story of God's faithfulness and lovingkindness to the people of Israel. Rewrite the psalm in your own words to tell the story of God's faithful love to your family.[8]

Day 4
Being Teachable

Gentleness, in our culture, feels like weakness. But as we learn about being gentle, it's fascinating to see that Jesus—the Man we all want to become like—was described as gentle, meek, and lowly in heart.

Take up my yoke and learn from me, because I am lowly and humble in heart, and you will find rest for your souls.
MATTHEW 11:29

Tell Daughter Zion, "See, your King is coming to you, gentle, and mounted on a donkey, and on a colt, the foal of a donkey."
MATTHEW 21:5

Now I Paul, myself, appeal to you by the meekness and gentleness of Christ—I who am humble among you in person but bold toward you when absent.
2 CORINTHIANS 10:1

Do you see the power in being gentle and the strength it takes to do so?

As parents, we have the privilege of modeling for our kids how to use our power, but that power begins with submission. In other words, the action of gentleness requires an attitude of humility, or a willingness to submit to the Holy Spirit.

Practically, this means that we show our kids the importance of remaining teachable, especially when we see them being impatient with letting others have a turn, throwing a fit if they lose a game, or allowing their emotions to get the best of them with a sibling.

In what areas are your kids teachable, especially as it relates to loving others?

Where do they have a difficult time being teachable? How can you help them learn to be teachable in these areas?

Read Proverbs 18:2.

How does this apply to being gentle toward others?

Is your tendency to listen to others or get your point across first?

Pay attention to the moments when your kids think life isn't fair, or you see resentment build up because they feel wronged. Use this opportunity to talk to them about how they would feel if someone else acted that way toward them (Matt. 7:12).

Talk about how they could respond differently—more gently. Help them understand how to catch themselves in teachable moments like these, looking out "not only for his own interests, but also for the interests of others" (Phil. 2:4).

Read John 21:1-19.

How was Jesus gentle toward Peter following the resurrection?

What did Jesus specifically do to show Peter that He understood Peter's story?

 **Application**

MORNING PRAYER

Heavenly Father, instill in my children a teachable spirit. Give them insight into their own feelings and reactions.

DINNERTIME STORY

Tell your kids about a moment you felt proud of them for being gentle with someone, especially when the other person wasn't very kind toward them. What specifically did they do to show gentleness?

BEDTIME QUESTION

What does it mean to be gentle? Do you think it's difficult being gentle toward others?

ACTIVITY

A Gentle Travel in Time: Let your kids talk about a time they wish they had been gentler in how they responded to someone. For instance, I (Josh) remember when my sister made fun of me for mispronouncing the name of a gas station. She laughed really hard. Instead of making light of the situation and seeing the silliness of my own mistake, I got really defensive. I brought up words she said incorrectly and angrily picked back at her. Instead of having a moment when we laughed together at ourselves, my defensiveness turned it into a big ole angry mess.

Use this activity as an opportunity to reflect on a time when you wish you had responded to someone differently, especially more gently. Use these scenarios not to beat yourselves up, but to learn from them for how you can humble yourselves and be more gentle in the future. To add a new level to the activity, role-play the scenario as if it is happening again, and explore how you, or your kids, would handle it differently.

Day 5
Being Faithful to What Matters Most

As a dad, I (Josh) have to confess that too often I get my priorities mixed up. Though I'm mostly aware of how I spend my time, I can be unfaithful at times to the things I need to be faithful in.

I had a moment not long ago when Christi challenged me about our marriage. She asked why we were growing distant and why I wasn't being very loving in how I spoke to her. I couldn't believe the accusation. I truly hadn't even noticed. In fact, I thought we were doing pretty well!

Little did I realize it took that moment for me to wake up to how I was prioritizing my loyalties and allowing work and uncontrollable circumstances to own my thought life. I took Christi, and our marriage, for granted. Even though I was physically present, I wasn't emotionally available to her.

Though it took a few days to mentally and emotionally reset my priorities and surrender my concerns to the Lord, I had to apologize to Christi. I realized that I hadn't been fully present with our kids either.

To be fair, these are circumstances that can happen to any of us on a regular basis. But what happens if we continually fail to recognize how we're prioritizing our loyalties? If we don't remain faithful to God, today's needs will consume our hearts and minds.

Read Luke 18:1-8.

What did the persistent widow prioritize in her life?

One of the most alarming verses in all of Scripture is Luke 18:8. What do you need to consider in your own life as you read this verse in light of your own faith journey?

As you evaluate your own calendar and how you spend your time, to what would your kids say you are most faithful?

Are your children's sports, extracurricular activities, or the arts filtered through the lens of their faith, or is their faith just another activity on the schedule?

Begin by looking at your calendar. What do you give your time to? Dads, are you more loyal to your football team than you are to making sure your family is plugged in at church? Moms, are you more loyal to your to-do list than you are to playing with the kids? Parents, are you more faithful to your boss than you are to God? Or is God your CEO, guiding and leading your work on a regular basis, through ongoing prayer and regular Sabbath?

Look at your kids' calendar. What are you teaching them to be faithful to by how you lead your family?

In our culture, travel sports teams, good grades, and other extracurricular activities are the currency of the day. Are we so busy that we cannot see God in the midst of the frenzy?

One of the best activities for leading your family and evaluating your priorities is establishing family values. As you look at your calendar and what you give your heart to, consider the family values you established earlier in this study.

Do your family values match what your calendar says you value? If not, what can you do this week to help them better align?

 Application

MORNING PRAYER

Lord God, protect my children's future spouses, should they marry. Surround them with adults who produce the fruit of the Spirit in their everyday lives that they may see it lived out.

DINNERTIME STORY

Talk to your kids tonight about how Jesus was rejected and persecuted. Ask them how they think He felt. Tell them to use feeling words (alone, sad, scared, rejected, etc.). Talk to them about what He went through—being rejected by His Father in heaven, so that our Father in heaven would accept us (Matt. 27:46). Yet, He was without sin, gentle, meek, and "humble in heart" (Matt. 11:29). Talk about what Jesus might have been thinking. Who were His eyes fixed on?

BEDTIME QUESTION

Was there a moment when you got down on yourself this week? Tell me about that. When did you feel most proud (in a healthy way) of yourself this week?

ACTIVITY

Acts of Gentleness: Challenge your kids to be gentle with at least three different people who might push their buttons. For instance, if one of their siblings takes a toy or doesn't cooperate, ask them to explain how they were able to control their feelings of anger and respond with a gentle attitude.

You can even make a chart to help them. On the chart, label the date, the person who angered them, and how they responded in gentleness. The older your kids, the more conversation you can have about what went on inside them to act in gentleness. How did they want to react? What stopped them from reacting that way? You can even use this as a way to talk about the differences between reacting in anger and responding in gentleness.

And, Mom or Dad, don't be offended when the person who angers them is you. This is a great way to teach them to respond even to you in gentler ways!

Bonus Application

MORNING PRAYER

Lord God, I pray my children have a forgiving spirit and learn not to be easily offended.

DINNERTIME STORY

Tell your children about a time you felt rejected or put down by someone when you were in school. Did you respond in gentleness? If not, walk through with your kids what responding in gentleness might have looked like.

BEDTIME QUESTION

What's one thing we can do as a family after school, or on the weekend, that would brighten your day? What's one thing we could do for someone else that would brighten his or her day this weekend? How can we do that together?

ACTIVITY

Take Two. And Action! This is a game (or really two games in one) that helps teach our children how to build their identity in Christ and the truth of His Word. Identity, or self-acceptance, is more than an abstract sense of who we are; it is an action—and it begins with training our brains to think about ourselves in a certain way. For instance, signs of self-acceptance include when we take responsibility for our actions, stand up for our beliefs, pursue our passions, or do what we're good at. When our kids accept who they are, they are less likely to feel the need to defend themselves.

This activity can be turned into two games. For instance, you could play the first part with older kids or teens and the second part with both older, and especially, younger kids.

TAKE 1. Discuss either positive or negative messages about ourselves we picked up along the way. Everybody think of one message (you can make the game about positive or negative messages) that you or your kids picked up from another person. What message do you remember being told? Did that message stick? If so, how?

TAKE 2. Now take action and "be transformed by the renewing of your mind" (Rom. 12:2) by speaking truth about who God created you to be. What was the positive or negative message you or your child discovered? What does Scripture say about you that refutes or confirms the messages you picked up? Can you recite Bible passages that speak truth about who you are?

If you have younger kids, begin here. As part of Take 2, choose any of the following sentences to complete. Do this during drive time or any time throughout the day to help your kids instill in themselves the truth about who God made them to be. Feel free to add more.

- I am courageous. An example of a time when I was courageous is _____.
- I am confident in who God made me to be. A time when I stuck up for myself was _____.
- I am loved. People who love me for who I am include _____.
- I make mistakes and learn from them. An example of a time I made a mistake but made it right was _____.
- I'm allowed to be happy. A time when I was happy was _____.
- I am not alone. Someone who is there for me when I need them is _____.
- I am a good friend. A time when I was there for or encouraged a friend was _____.
- I show respect to others. A time when I showed respect to someone was _____.
- I make good decisions. A time when I made a good decision was _____.
- God made me with special gifts and strengths. One thing I am really good at is _____.

If you're playing this game with younger children who are too young to look up Scripture passages themselves to confirm the truth of who God sees them as, look up a few verses to read to them after the activity is over. Psalm 139; Ephesians 1; and 1 Peter 2 are great places to start.

Understanding My Child

Tie your discipline into teaching the Bible. The word *discipline* means, "to train." When your children misbehave, use biblical values as anchor points to train your children. In addition to the passages we can point our children to about obeying Mom and Dad (Eph. 6:1-3), what are some other biblical truths you want to highly value in your home (i.e. telling the truth, treating others with kindness, holding the tongue, etc.)?

Write down the top values you already instill in your home on a regular basis. What verse can you write next to it to train your child in the Word? For example, we use Philippians 2:3. When we're not sharing, this verse becomes the basis for our discipline and conversation.

1. How to Cultivate Faithfulness in Our Kids

How has God been faithful to you and your family?

Tell a story about a moment you felt proud of your kids for being faithful to God, especially when others may have been doing the wrong thing. What specifically did they do to walk in faithfulness?

Talk about your own spiritual journey growing in faithfulness. What has God been showing you about walking in faith as an adult?

How can you walk in concert with the Holy Spirit to teach and remind you of the things Jesus said about who He is?

2. What Is Gentleness?

Read Proverbs 15:1 and James 1:19-20 aloud.

What's required of us to be gentle?

What's the opposite response of gentleness?

In your own life, do you consider yourself generally gentle in response to others or angry when you feel wronged or not understood? Why?

Read Psalm 23 aloud as a group.

When have you experienced God as a gentle Shepherd? How has God gently cared for you in your walk with Him?

Have you seen gentleness as a strength or as a weakness?

3. How to Cultivate Gentleness in Our Kids

Read John 7:53–8:11 aloud.

What do you take away from this situation that applies to how you talk to your kids in their sin?

Read Matthew 5:5. When we've been wronged, we have power. How do you exert your power in these situations? Give an example.

What's difficult about forgiving someone?

How can you be gentler toward your spouse this week? Your kids? Be specific.

4. Being Teachable

Read Proverbs 18:2 aloud.

How does this apply to being gentle toward others?

Is your tendency to listen to others or get your point across first?

Read John 21:1-19 aloud.

How was Jesus gentle toward Peter following the resurrection?

What did Jesus specifically do to show Peter that He understood Peter's story?

5. Being Faithful to What Matters Most

Read Luke 18:1-8 aloud.

What did the persistent widow prioritize in her life?

One of the most alarming verses in all of Scripture is Luke 18:8. What do you need to consider in your own life as you read this verse in light of your own faith journey?

As you evaluate your own calendar and how you spend your time, to what would your kids say you're most faithful? Should that change?

A PERSON WITHOUT

self-control

IS LIKE A HOUSE

with its doors

AND WINDOWS

knocked out.

PROVERBS 25:28, THE MESSAGE

SESSION 6: SELF-CONTROL

*I now think of discipline as the continual everyday process
of helping a child learn self-discipline.*[1]
FRED ROGERS

As if it wasn't already difficult enough just to get your child to sit at the table for a full meal without getting up, to go a full day without the kids bickering at one another, or to get your teenager to put down the phone, cultivating kids to be self-controlled can feel absolutely impossible—and disheartening. The good news is twofold:

First, God will honor you as you cultivate your kids in the fruit of the Spirit. We know this because He honors those who are humble and submit to His will (Col. 3:23-24). And cultivating kids in the fruit of the Spirit requires that we humbly surrender our children to Him. Your surrender honors God. Can you imagine if you spent more time meditating on that truth instead of how you think you just messed up with your kids?

Secondly, you can't get your kids to be self-controlled anyway. Yes, you read that right. Self-control is a work of the Holy Spirit, not a work of the parent. If you want to raise self-controlled kids, your job is to lead them into a deepening relationship with Jesus, where the Holy Spirit refines their character. No matter if research can measure it or not, this is why prayer is the most effective parenting strategy on the planet.

The Greek word for self-control in Galatians 5:23 is *egkráteia*, and means self-mastery or "dominion within."[2] We love that phrase, "dominion within." In other words, self-control is what proceeds out from what's already within a person. If the flesh has dominion within us, what proceeds out is selfish pride, anger, and jealousy (Gal. 5:19-21). If the Holy Spirit has dominion within us, what proceeds out is "love, joy, peace, patience, kindness, goodness, faithfulness, gentleness, and self-control" (Gal. 5:22-23).

Self-control keeps our conscience clean. With that in mind, we can set the temperature, moisture, and environment of our parenting greenhouse to be conducive for self-control to grow in five ways:

1. Set the emotional climate of your home
2. Delay gratification
3. Deal thoroughly with sin
4. Discover triggers
5. Play the movie to the end

Day 1

Set the Emotional Climate of Your Home

Children go through a lot of change growing up. New friends. New schools. New homes. New routines. New siblings. If you move to a new city, they get a new home, a new church, and an entirely new peer group. This is the positive.

When there's change, there's also loss: losing friendships, the memories of a childhood home, or even the loss of loved ones. With all of this change comes a lot of emotion.

As we seek to cultivate self-control in our kids, we need to remember that self-control is most difficult when we're overwhelmed with emotion—especially emotions that our kids cannot label or understand.

That's why self-control is best cultivated in an environment of love, not fear.[3] Fear overrides the part of our brain responsible for self-control (the prefrontal cortex). In other words, when we're overwhelmed by fear, we often can't think straight. Solving problems and making rational decisions is much more difficult.

This is why toddlers throw temper tantrums. They can't access the prefrontal cortex. Emotions felt for the first time can be incredibly overwhelming. However, as our children grow in the Lord, the Holy Spirit can work in and through us as parents to help our kids label their emotions.

If you remember from Session 3, our presence literally has a calming effect on our child's brain. When they feel negative emotion—anger, jealousy, sadness, fear—our ability as a parent to lead in grace, validate the feeling, and not shame them for it provides the peace needed for our children to put words to what they feel.

Putting words to what they feel settles their brains long enough to discern how to respond to a situation, not react to it. In other words, our child's emotions should be yield signs, not green lights. In contrast, a lack of self-control is when our kids act on their emotions.

Do you tend to react to your negative emotions, allowing them to guide your actions, or would you describe yourself as someone who responds to your emotions?

Name one way your parents were emotionally safe for you.

What's one way your parents weren't emotionally safe for you?

There's no question that children need the power of the Holy Spirit to be self-controlled. But the Holy Spirit doesn't just take over and do that for them. We all build the endurance through discipleship and sanctification. We can help our children recognize their emotions, help them slow them down to think about why they feel the way they do, and then work with them to problem solve for the appropriate actions.

Of course, discipling our kids to be self-controlled is challenging because it requires that we, too, be self-controlled.

When has fear, anger, sadness, or jealousy prevented you from having self-control?

What do you wish you had done differently looking back on the situation?

We all lack self-control at times with our kids. What one way can you begin modeling for your children how to exhibit self-control?

What one strategy can you and your spouse implement to show self-control in front of your kids as it relates to your marriage?

Read Titus 2 aloud.

What behaviors are consistent with being self-controlled?

Older men (v. 2):

Older women (vv. 3-5):

Young men (vv. 6-8):

Young women (vv. 4-5):

Employees (vv. 9-10):

What are the benefits of being self-controlled according to this passage?

When you read the Greek definition of the word *self-controlled* to mean "dominion within" in the introduction, what came to mind for you?

 Application

MORNING PRAYER

Heavenly Father, I come into agreement with Your Spirit to ask that my children become self-controlled in everything, making themselves examples "of good works with integrity and dignity in your teaching" (Titus 2:6-7).

DINNERTIME STORY

Talk about a moment you showed self-control even though you were scared (i.e. standing up to a bully, giving a speech, telling a friend how he or she hurt you, singing in front of a crowd, losing a game but being a good sport, etc.).

BEDTIME QUESTION

What does it mean to have self-control? When did you feel most proud of yourself this week for controlling your feelings or behavior? Tell me about that.

ACTIVITY

The Oreo® Game![4] Put an Oreo or something delicious in front of your kids for the car ride or after they wake up. Tell your kids that they can eat the one Oreo now or if they can wait until the destination or a certain time of day, they will get a surprise. You can either reveal it will be two Oreos or you could simply tell them they'll "receive a surprise for waiting." Talk to your kids about why it was hard to wait or why they chose not to wait.

Day 2
Delay Gratification

In *Safe House: How Emotional Safety Is the Key to Raising Kids Who Live, Love, and Lead Well*, I (Josh) wrote about one of the most fascinating studies on human behavior.

In the study, Walter Mischel and his colleagues offered preschool children their choice of a marshmallow, an Oreo, or a pretzel stick. The kids were told they could eat their chosen treat right then—or if they waited fifteen minutes, they could receive two treats. The kids had to contemplate whether to eat the Oreo now or wait a short while and have two Oreos.

Sound familiar? If you did this activity with your child on Day 1, how did it turn out? Could you be that patient?

After following these children for the next twenty years, the child's decision that day to simply eat an Oreo or wait and receive two of them proved to have profound implications. The children who chose to delay gratification turned out to get better grades in school and had higher SAT scores when they became teenagers. Even as they matured into adults, they proved to be physically healthier, professionally more competent, and able to stay committed in romantic relationships.[5]

When our kids can hold off on the impulse to *feel better* in the moment, it opens the door to living, loving, and leading better in the long run. Put off playing with friends to study for a test and you'll likely get better grades. Hold off on that cookie and you eat fewer empty calories.

Use some of the suggested activities this week to help your children delay gratification. Instead of buying them a toy right away, ask them to wait anywhere from a day or a week depending on their age and the price of the toy. Direct them to withhold money or their allowance to save for something special. Reward them for showing self-control and restraint.

What's most difficult for you as a parent when it comes to withholding or delaying gratification from your kids?

What happens when you do? How do your kids respond in the short-term? What about a week or more later?

Read Nehemiah 4.

What was Nehemiah's response to being laughed at?

Notice Nehemiah's active waiting by pursuing the Lord in prayer (v. 9). If you were laughed at or talked about, how would you react? Or how would you respond?

How can you more effectively pray when you lack self-control in a situation?

Read Luke 4:1-13. Reread verse 8:

> *And Jesus answered him [Satan], "It is written:*
> *Worship the Lord your God, and serve him only."*
> **LUKE 4:8**

In what ways was Satan trying to get Jesus to give in to temptation?

In which of these areas would you have trouble with self-control?

How did Jesus stand firm? What were His tactics to maintain self-control and not give in to the temptation?

 Application

MORNING PRAYER

Holy Spirit, fill my children as You did Jesus going into the wilderness. Give my children Your power to be self-controlled when they are most tempted (Luke 4:1-2).

DINNERTIME STORY

Tell your kids about a moment you felt proud of them for showing self-control. What specifically did they do?

BEDTIME QUESTION

When did you let your emotions get the best of you today? What could you have done differently?

ACTIVITY

The Goodie Box: Go to a dollar store and buy a handful of goodies to put into a box. Allow your children to choose a toy from the box whenever you catch them displaying self-control in a way that makes you proud (not interrupting a conversation, not whining or complaining to be done eating, etc.).

Day 3
Deal Thoroughly with Sin

As we raise our kids and grow in the Holy Spirit ourselves, God is teaching us sin's role in keeping us from walking intimately with Him.

A. W. Tozer, wrote that one of the five keys to a deeper spiritual life is to deal thoroughly with sin.[6] In other words, we need to ruthlessly rid anything from our lives that would hinder our relationship with Jesus.

One of the ways we do this with our kids is figuratively taking them to the cross when they sin. For example, when they disobey what we ask them to do, after their consequence, we pray together. We have our kids verbally ask Jesus to forgive them. If they don't know what to pray, we have them repeat after us.

We go to the cross, too, especially when we wrong our kids. We'll sit together, seek the forgiveness of our kids, and then pray to God to forgive our sins as well. Then we ask for God's grace as we talk to our kids about how we'll make the situation right.

That's because sin ensnares us and keeps us from walking intimately with Christ.

Read Hebrews 12:1-2.

Is there a hindrance or sin that has "dominion within," keeping your eyes from being on Jesus?

What steps have you taken to gain control of it?

Is there someone you need to talk to for the sake of running with endurance and not allowing shame to keep you from walking fully in the Holy Spirit?

Read Romans 6:15-23.

What does this passage say about control? Can we really ever be free from being controlled by anything?

Reread verses 21-22.

What do you see in your kids hindering them from walking closely with Jesus?

How can you love your kids through it and show them how their sin leads to death?

Define *sanctification*.

Sanctification is the term for growing in likeness to God. We'll be growing in our sanctification our whole lives as we learn to be more and more like Christ in our thoughts and actions.

Dealing thoroughly with sin, we have found, especially for our children, includes generational strongholds that need to be cut off.

Read Exodus 20:5-6.

We all have areas that need pruning. Write down one or two areas in your life where you struggle with self-control.

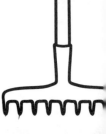

How have you seen it manifested in the generations prior to you?

Are there any other generational strongholds you can think of hindering you from running the race with endurance?

Ask God to reveal where He is working in your life. Do you tend to yell when your kids are disobedient? Do you lack self-control with your spouse in how you speak to or treat him or her? Or maybe it's in a different area of your life like a habitual sin or being a workaholic.

Choose to relentlessly cut off anything that could hinder your children. We have done this and still find things come up from time to time.

Remember, our kids model who we are. Put a stake in the ground with us today, declare self-control as your strength, and invoke the Holy Spirit's influence onto your children and children's children for generations to come.

 Application

MORNING PRAYER
Lord Jesus, give my children the self-control they need not to give into peer pressure.

DINNERTIME STORY
Tell your kids about a disappointment you had to overcome this week. How did you get through it?

BEDTIME QUESTION
When do you have the most difficult time controlling yourself (i.e. not getting what you want, when your sibling takes a toy, eating dessert, etc.)?

ACTIVITY

Waiting Games: Interestingly, the word *wait* in the Bible is a verb. It means "to expect." In the instance of Simeon and Anna (Luke 2:25-38), the word means that they expected the coming of the first advent, or the birth of baby Jesus. They knew without a doubt, Jesus was coming. Used in other places in the New Testament, this word *wait* is used to focus on our daily walk with God, as we expectantly wait for the second Advent, the second coming of Jesus.

For today's activity, think about what it means to wait. For example, begin by asking your kids how they feel in the final days leading up to Christmas? Why do they feel this way? They know it's coming, right!? We do Advent calendars to count down for this very reason. But could you imagine being Simeon and Anna? They knew Christmas, or the birth of Jesus, was coming, but they didn't know when. How would it change how we feel if we knew Christmas was coming, but we didn't know when? How would it change how your kids feel leading up to Christmas if they didn't know when it was coming? When we have to wait for things, people, or events, how do we handle it? What does it say about our hearts?

Jesus is coming again! We are waiting on His return. But we, too, don't know when. Tell your kids to make two columns on a piece of paper. Join in if you so dare. On the left column write, *Ways I wait poorly.* On the right column write, *Ways I can wait expectantly.* Think through scenarios like waiting in line, waiting in traffic, waiting for Christmas, waiting for school or work to let out, waiting to take turns, and so forth.

This exercise helps us to see on paper how we can better honor God in our waiting. When we act as though Jesus is coming back, our daily wait, like Simeon's and Anna's, will be worth it. Talk about ways you can wait without being bummed out, but thanking God with expectation.

Day 4
Discover Triggers

Sometimes our own lack of self-control manifests itself in our closest relationships. The trouble is, we don't always have the ability to see it in ourselves. Answering the following questions will require humility, but if we want to grow in the Spirit, we need to crucify our flesh (Gal. 5:24).

Where have you seen a lack of self-control in your relationships with loved ones (being short with how you speak, passive aggressive, raising your voice, etc.)?

Write down a situation or specific scenario when you talked back or spoke in a harsh tone of voice toward your spouse, kids, parents, or loved one.

What triggered your response? Were you angry? Did you feel rejected? Forgotten? Perhaps you felt taken advantage of because you felt as though that person didn't pull his or her weight in your relationship. Or maybe you were overwhelmed with life's circumstances and you spoke from a place of exhaustion. Write down a list of what triggers a reaction in you.

If you can, do this exercise with someone in your group who knows you well. Sometimes we see something in one another we can't see in ourselves. Ask the Holy Spirit to increase the strength you need to produce the fruit of self-control. If you're married, talk to your spouse about the fruit you would like to see increased in your life.

For instance, maybe you need patience so that you may not be as quick to react. Perhaps you need gentleness in how you respond.

Write down one or two characteristics of the fruit of the Spirit you would like to grow in and ask God to cultivate those in you. Also, to soften your heart toward others, begin praying and asking God to show you how He sees those around you—your spouse, your kids, your family, your neighbors (Eph. 5:22-33; Col. 3:18-23; 1 Pet. 3:1-8).

When you have a lack of self-control with your kids, what triggers it? Is it the end of the day, when you're tired? After your kids have repeatedly not listened to what you told them to do? When they are nagging with constant "Daddy, Daddy, Daddy," or "Mommy, Mommy, Mommy?"

Write down what triggers a reaction in you with your kids.

What can you do to eliminate or decrease these reactions in these moments?

Application

MORNING PRAYER
Father, give my child self-control in how he or she speaks to others (Prov. 18:21).

DINNERTIME STORY
Tell your kids about some of your favorite moments you've spent with them. Let them hear from you what you love doing with them.

BEDTIME QUESTION
Name one person who always seems to put you in a good mood. Who do you like being around? Why do you like being around them?

ACTIVITY
"Bored" Games: Play a board game as a family (without screens). However, choose one that may take a little longer than they can sit still for. Monopoly® may be good for teenagers. For us, Chutes and Ladders® is enough to test our steadfastness. Tell your children to stick the game out until the end, especially if they're losing or bored. Talk to them about what it means to be steadfast and self-controlled, no matter how they feel about what or how they're doing (like losing the game).

And if being a sore loser is an issue in your home (like it is in ours), use this lesson to show your kids that selfishness is not a fruit of the Spirit. God cares more about how we win or lose than if we win or lose.

Afterward, have some bread together as a snack. Use butter, jam, or even Nutella®. Make it taste really good. Use this as an experiential lesson that Jesus, who is our Bread of life, cares not only about what we go through, but how we act going through it. When we feel out of control, we can turn to Him to give us what we need to be self-controlled.

Day 5
Play the Movie to the End

Children tend to have a difficult time using hindsight and foresight. So do teenagers for that matter, making them more likely to be impulsive both in words and actions.

Using Proverbs 25:28 as a visual, direct your kids to learn how to play the movie forward. Whenever your kids have a difficult situation or decision in front of them, tell them to picture themselves in a movie. Who is the character they want to portray? If they were to seek revenge on a friend, let them discuss how it would likely play out. How would the friend feel? How would your child feel? What would be the long-lasting effects of that decision? Try varying scenarios.

Read Luke 2:36-37.

> *There was also a prophetess, Anna, a daughter of Phanuel, of the tribe of Asher. She was well along in years, having lived with her husband seven years after her marriage, and was a widow for eighty-four years. She did not leave the temple, serving God night and day with fasting and prayers.*
> **LUKE 2:36-37**

Anna was well along in years. She was widowed after only seven years of marriage. Can you imagine the heartache and grief as a young woman? Though Anna could have grown bitter or resentful, she chose to seek God and "play the movie forward." The Bible says she was in the temple both day and night. She wasn't out gossiping with her girlfriends or moping around about being alone—a focus only on how she felt in the moment.

Instead, Anna knew the importance of godly friends and community for what was to come. She sought God at the temple and hung out there. Anna, like Simeon (vv. 25-35), grew to wait patiently on God, even in her distress.

Anna actively pursued God while she waited for him. Her waiting wasn't like we think of waiting today. We grow bored. Look at our phones. Watch TV. Anna instead fasted and

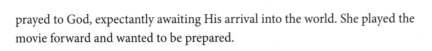

prayed to God, expectantly awaiting His arrival into the world. She played the movie forward and wanted to be prepared.

And because she did, Anna was in the temple the same day as Simeon, who also waited for the coming King. Anna recognized when Mary and Joseph entered with Jesus. The Bible tells us that when Anna saw the baby, she walked over to Jesus, thanked God, and began telling everyone about Him. Her wait was worth it.

What do you do to actively wait (verb) on things to come? Or do you tend to wait by not doing anything productive or helpful?

Verse 37 says that Anna fasted and prayed. Fasting is a spiritual discipline that requires a lot of self-control!

Have you ever fasted? If so, how long, and what did you fast from?

How often do you fast?

Fasting and praying help us to actively wait on the Lord. Teach your kids what it means to fast. Consider planting in them a desire to fast and pray by doing it regularly yourself. They could fast from something other than food. They could abstain from screens or sweets for a period of time instead.

Read Daniel 1:8-21. Notice the first part of verse 8:

> *Daniel <u>determined</u> that he would not defile himself*
> *with the king's food or with the wine he drank.*
> **DANIEL 1:8a, emphasis added**

Do you think it was difficult for Daniel to remain steadfast and determined in his decision? What might have made it difficult for him to remain self-controlled?

What can you do today to be active in your pursuit of Jesus, so that you'd recognize His voice?

How can you pass this discipline onto your kids?

Application

MORNING PRAYER

Dear Lord, give me insight and discernment for my children. Show me the areas (food, competition, emotions, and so forth) I need to be aware of to provide covering for my children to be self-controlled.

DINNERTIME STORY

Tell your kids about one of the boldest prayers you ever prayed and how God answered it. How long did it take Him to answer? Did you have to wait and be self-controlled? What did that look like?

BEDTIME QUESTION

What's a big prayer you want to begin asking of God?

ACTIVITY

That's Not Fair! Role-play with your kids tonight to show them what jealousy looks like. If you have multiple children, direct them to sit at the table. Give one child an iPad to play with, one child a boring book, one child a toy, and so on. Make sure to distribute the toys in a way you know will cause your kids to argue or not control their emotions. If you have one child, make him or her do something boring while you do something fun.

Let them play a little bit. Study their behavior. After a few minutes, process with your kids what they felt. Who is whining? Is anybody in a fit of rage? Did anyone try to sabotage and take another's toy? Talk about jealousy with your children in this role-play. Use it as an opportunity to talk about self-control. Brainstorm with your kids ways they can act differently when they start to feel jealous or that life isn't fair.

Do the same activity again, but this time tell them they get to rotate the toys after five minutes. Was there a behavior change?

Bonus Application

MORNING PRAYER

Father, like Daniel, who was determined not to defile himself by eating the king's food, give my kids self-control for Your glory (Dan. 1:8a).

DINNERTIME STORY

Tell your kids the greatest lesson you learned going through this study. Invite them into your spiritual journey of growing in the fruit of the Spirit. As a family, talk about a new tradition, practice, or activity you will implement to grow together over time.

BEDTIME QUESTION

What's one way we could go out of our way to serve another family this weekend?

ACTIVITY

God's Plan Is Better. Have your children grab some money. If they already have a dollar bill or some change in their pockets, even better. Put a five or ten dollar bill up your sleeve, but don't let your kids see it. Ask them to give you the dollar or change they have in their pocket. Tell them they'll never see it again but to give it to you anyway because you need it. Ask if they're willing to give it up. Do they trust you? Praise their willingness to sacrifice it once they give it away. Have them now sit at the table. Walk over and give them the five or ten dollars you had up your sleeve.

Use this as an object lesson to show your kids that you would never ask them to sacrifice something if you didn't have something that's better for them. In a similar way, God always does what is best for His plans and purposes, and we can always trust Him.

Tell a story of how you sacrificed something in your life and got more in return than you ever imagined possible. Make sure to emphasize that our returns are not always bigger amounts of what we gave up; sometimes they are disguised or even unknown. Were you self-controlled in your sacrifice and waiting? Share honestly about your experience of being self-controlled in such situations. Be sure to talk about the fruit you saw grow because of the situation—joy, patience, faith in God, a closer relationship to Jesus, self-control, and so forth. You can also talk about earthly sacrifices and self-control we must have for greater purposes (athletics, graduate degrees, missionaries, doctors, having children, etc.).

Understanding My Child

Focus on building your relationship with your children. Cultivating the fruit of the Spirit is as much about the time we spend with our kids as it is about reading the Bible. Don't force more than your kids can consume each week. Also, don't put unnecessary guilt on yourself for not covering a specific number of Bible chapters or verses. Your time together will quickly fizzle out this way. Instead, focus on having fun and becoming a student of your child.

As you navigate through your time together with your child, ask questions about their spiritual journey. You can ask questions like: *What is God teaching you this week? Are you burdened for someone (a sick friend, a sibling, etc.)? What are you most grateful for this week (1 Thess. 5:18)? How are you experiencing the joy of your salvation (Ps. 51:12)? What are you struggling with right now? What does the Bible say about this struggle (Ps. 46:1)? Do you have sin for which you need to confess and repent (1 John 1:9)? What's one way you can become more like Jesus this week (Eph. 5:1-2)?*

1. Set the Emotional Climate of Your Home

Read Titus 2 aloud.

What behaviors are consistent with being self-controlled? Make a list.

Older men (Titus 2:2):

Older women (vv. 3-5):

Young men (vv. 6-8):

Young women (vv. 4-5):

Employees (vv. 9-10):

What are the benefits of being self-controlled according to this passage?

When you read the Greek definition of the word *self-controlled* to mean "dominion within," what came to mind for you?

How do you tend to react or respond when you feel controlled by something or someone?

2. Delay Gratification

What's most difficult for you as a parent when it comes to withholding or delaying gratification from your kids?

What happens when you do? How do your kids respond in the short-term? What about a week or more later?

Read Luke 4:1-13 aloud.

In what ways was Satan trying to get Jesus to give in to temptation?

In which of these areas would you have trouble with self-control?

How did Jesus stand firm? What were His tactics to maintain self-control and not give in to the temptation?

3. Deal Thoroughly with Sin

Read Hebrews 12:1-2 aloud.

How can our group help one another run with endurance?

Read Romans 6:15-23 aloud.

What does this passage say about control? Can we really ever be free from being controlled by anything?

What do you see in your kids that hinders them from walking closely with Jesus?

4. Discover Triggers

What characteristics of the fruit would you like to grow in?

What triggers a reaction in you with your kids? What can you do to eliminate or decrease these reactions in these moments?

5. Play the Movie to the End

What do you do to actively wait (verb) on things to come? Or do you tend to wait by not doing anything productive or helpful?

Read Daniel 1:8-21.

What made it difficult for Daniel to remain self-controlled?

Share a decision of self-control you made that you look on with fondness because you were determined not to allow emotions to get in the way of the outcome.

What's one takeaway you'll continue to use from this study?

Introducing Your Child to Christ

Your most significant calling and privilege as a parent is to introduce your children to Jesus Christ. A good way to begin this conversation is to tell them about your own faith journey.

Outlined below is a simple gospel presentation you can share with your child. Define any terms they don't understand and make it more conversational, letting the Spirit guide your words and allowing your child to ask questions and contribute along the way.

GOD RULES. The Bible tells us God created everything, and He's in charge of everything. (See Gen. 1:1; Col. 1:16-17; Rev. 4:11.)

WE SINNED. We all choose to disobey God. The Bible calls this sin. Sin separates us from God and deserves God's punishment of death. (See Rom. 3:23; 6:23.)

GOD PROVIDED. God sent Jesus, the perfect solution to our sin problem, to rescue us from the punishment we deserve. It's something we, as sinners, could never earn on our own. Jesus alone saves us. (See John 3:16; Eph. 2:8-9.)

JESUS GIVES. He lived a perfect life, died on the cross for our sins, and rose again. Because Jesus gave up His life for us, we can be welcomed into God's family for eternity. This is the best gift ever! (See Rom. 5:8; 2 Cor. 5:21; Eph. 2:8-9; 1 Pet. 3:18.)

WE RESPOND. Believe in your heart that Jesus alone saves you through what He's already done on the cross. Repent, by turning away from your sin. Tell God and others that your faith is in Jesus. (See John 14:6; Rom. 10:9-10,13.)

If your child is ready to respond, explain what it means for Jesus to be Lord of his or her life. Guide your child in prayer to repent and express his or her belief in Jesus. If your child responds in faith, celebrate! You now have the opportunity to disciple your child to be more like Christ.

ENDNOTES

Session 1

1. Dr. James Strong, "*Nouthesía*," G3559, *The New Strong's Exhaustive Concordance of the Bible*. Available online at www.blueletterbible.org.

2. R. Epstein, "What Makes a Good Parent? A Scientific Analysis Ranks the 10 Most Effective Child-Rearing Practices," *Journal of Lifelong Faith*, Vol. 5 Issue 3, (Fall 2011), 3-7.

3. Brené Brown, *Daring Greatly* (New York: Penguin Random House, 2012), 217.

4. John Gottman and Joan DeClaire, *The Heart of Parenting: How to Raise an Emotionally Intelligent Child* (New York: Simon & Schuster, 1997).

5. Josh Straub, *Safe House: How Emotional Safety Is the Key to Raising Kids Who Live, Love, and Lead Well* (Colorado Springs: WaterBrook, 2015), 31.

6. Jim Rohn, as quoted in Maarten van Doorn, "You Are The Average Of The Five People You Spend The Most Time With," *The Polymath Project* (Jun 20, 2018). Available online at https://medium.com.

7. Straub, *Safe House*.

8. Ibid.

Session 2

1. Robert A. Johnson, *The Fisher King and the Handless Maiden* (New York, HarperCollins, 1993), 6.

2. Straub, 20.

3. Daniel J. Siegel, M.D., and Tina Payne Bryson, Ph.D., *No-Drama Discipline* (New York: Bantam Books, 2016), xxiv.

4. Straub, 20.

5. Adapted from Dr. Tim Clinton and Dr. Joshua Straub, *God Attachment: Why You Believe, Act, and Feel the Way You Do About God* (New York: Howard Books, 2010).

6. Andy Andrews, *The Traveler's Gift* (Nashville, TN: Thomas Nelson, 2002), 108.

7. Brené Brown, *Daring Greatly: How the Courage to Be Vulnerable Transforms the Way We Live, Love, Parent, and Lead* (New York: Gotham Books, 2013), 124–125.

8. Ibid.

9. Ibid.

Session 3

1. Melissa Petruzzello, "Where Did the Peace Sign Come From?" *Encyclopedia Britannica*, online. Accessed 8 Jan 2019. Available at britannica.com.

2. Doug Hershey, *The Christian's Biblical Guide to Understanding Israel: Insight Into God's Heart for His People* (Lake Mary, FL: Creation House Books, 2011), 17.

3. John W. Ritenbaugh, "The Fruit of the Spirit: Peace," Forerunner, "Personal," May 1998. Available at www.bibletools.org.

4. Adapted from Stefanie's "5 Ways to Teach Gratitude to Children," *Simple Acres* blog. Available at https://simpleacresblog.com.

5. Ibid, Ritenbaugh.

6. Kay Arthur, "Illustration of Peace" in "Luke 2 Commentary," Precept Austin. Accessed 8 Jan 2019. Available at www.preceptaustin.org/pdf/61895.

7. Albert Barnes, "Commentary on Ephesians 6:4," *Barnes' Notes on the New Testament*. Available at www.studylight.org/commentary/ephesians/6-4.html.

8. Josh and Christi Straub, Interview with Dr. John Townsend, "#68: [Best Of Series Part 3] How To Not Raise Entitled Kids With Dr. John Townsend" *In This Together* podcast audio, August 1, 2018. Available at www.joshuastraub.com.

9. Jerry Rice, as quoted online at www.jerryricefootball.com/about.

Session 4

1. Josh Straub, "The Power of Kindness," *Focus on the Family* blog. Available at www.focusonthefamily.com.

2. Ibid.

3. Adapted from Josh Straub, "Finding Goodness," *Focus on the Family* blog. Available at www.focusonthefamily.com.

4. John Gottman and Nan Silver, *The Seven Principles for Making Marriage Work: A Practical Guide from the Country's Foremost Relationship Expert* (New York: Harmony Publishers, 2015), 260-276.

Session 5

1. "4240," HELPS Word-Studies. Available at https://biblehub.com/greek/4240.htm

2. Elizabeth Agnew Cochran, *Receptive Human Virtues: A New Reading of Jonathan Edwards's Ethics* (University Park, PA: The Pennsylvania State University Press, 2011).

3. "4239," HELPS Word-Studies. Available at https://biblehub.com/greek/4239.htm.

4. "Magnanimous," Dictionary.com. Unabridged based on the *Random House Unabridged Dictionary*, © Random House, Inc. 2019.

5. "Johnny Appleseed," by John Chapman (1774-1845), public domain.

6. A.W. Tozer, *Five Vows for Spiritual Power* (A Tozer Book, 2013), 9.

7. Adapted from Josh Straub, "Handle With Care," *Focus on the Family* blog. Available at www.focusonthefamily.com.

8. Adapted from "Sing to the Lord another new Psalm," Kids of Integrity, Focus on the Family. Available at www. kidsofintegrity.com/lessons/faithfulness/ hands-options.

Session 6

1. Fred Rogers and Barry Head, *Mister Rogers Talks With Parents* (Pittsburgh, PA: Family Communications, Inc., 1983), 150.

2. "1466," HELPS Word-Studies. BibleHub online. Available at https://biblehub.com/ greek/1466.htm.

3. Josh Straub, *Safe House.*

4. "The Oreo Game" is based on Walter Mischel's experiment in 1960 called "The Marshmallow Test." He later wrote a book on it entitled *The Marshmallow Test: Why Self-Control Is the Engine of Success* (New York: Little, Brown and Company, 2014).

5. Walter Mischel, Ebbe B. Ebbesen, and Antonette Raskoff Zeiss, "Cognitive and Attentional Mechanisms in Delay of Gratification," *Journal of Personality and Social Psychology 21,* no. 2 (February 1972): 204–218; Walter Mischel, Yuichi Shoda, and Monica L. Rodriguez, "Delay of Gratification in Children," *Science 244,* no. 4907 (May 26, 1989): 933–938; Walter Mischel and Ozlem Ayduk, "Willpower in a Cognitive-Affective Processing System: The Dynamics of Delay of Gratification," in *Handbook of Self-Regulation: Research, Theory, and Applications,* ed. Roy F. Baumeister and Kathleen D. Vohs (New York: Guilford, 2004), 99–129; Ozlem N. Ayduk, Rodolfo Mendoa-Denton, Walter Mischel, Geraldine Downey, Philip K. Peake, and Monica L. Rodriguez, "Regulating the Interpersonal Self: Strategic Self-Regulation for Coping with Rejection Sensitivity," *Journal of Personality and Social Psychology 79,* no. 5 (2000): 776–792; Tanya R. Schlam, Nicole L. Wilson, Yuichi Shoda, Walter Mischel, and Ozlem Ayduk, "Preschoolers' Delay of Gratification Predicts Their Body Mass 30 Years Later," *Journal of Pediatrics 162* (2013): 90–93; and Yuichi Shoda, Walter Mischel, Philip K. Peake, "Predicting Adolescent Cognitive and Self-Regulatory Competencies from Preschool Delay of Gratification: Identifying Diagnostic Conditions," *Developmental Psychology 26,* no. 6 (1990): 978–986.

6. A. W. Tozer, "Five Vows for Spiritual Power," *Gems from Tozer: Selections from the Writings of A. W. Tozer* (Camp Hill, PA: Christian Publications, 1969).

"Josh provides a road map for making our homes the emotionally safest places in the world for our kids."

—CANDACE CAMERON BURE, actress, author, producer, and mom

You don't need to do all the "right" things as a parent. Both science and the Bible show us that the most important thing we can provide for our kids is a place of emotional safety.

In *Safe House,* Dr. Straub moves beyond parenting techniques to help you develop a posture of parenting. He draws from his extensive research and personal experience to help you:

- *Understand how the culture is affecting your child and what you can do about it*
- *Discipline in a way that builds relationship*
- *Establish an unshakeable sense of faith, morality, and values in your home*
- *Feel more confident and peaceful as a parent*
- *And much more!*

MULTNOMAH

BECAUSE OUR WORLD NEEDS KIDS WHO CAN EMPATHIZE WITH OTHERS.

In a world where kids are dealing with everything from sibling rivalry to bullying, divorce to tragedy, *What Am I Feeling?* offers a biblically grounded way for children to verbalize their feelings, develop empathy and self-control, and understand their wonderful God-given emotions.

THIS BOOK PROVIDES THE BUILDING BLOCKS FOR A LIFETIME OF LOVING GOD AND LOVING OTHERS.

BONUS!

Also includes a pull-out feelings chart for your wall!

Includes a pull-out feelings chart!

WHAT AM I FEELING?

Dr. Josh and Christi Straub
Illustrations by Jane Butler

The Top 5 Struggles for Parents

1. THERE'S NEVER ANY TIME.

2. MY KIDS WON'T LISTEN.

3. I FEEL INADEQUATE.

4. I LOSE MY PATIENCE.

5. HOW DO I DISCIPLE MY KIDS?

Can you relate?

As parents, we all struggle with this list.

But do you want to know a secret?

It doesn't have to be this way. You shouldn't have to struggle with this list in order to raise your children well.

That's why we created 22:6 Parenting—a digital subscription that gives you monthly tools to teach your kids about Jesus.

With 22:6 Parenting, you get discipleship tools you can easily apply with your kids, coaching that encourages you as a parent, and community that supports you along the way.